"True Faith Works"

James
Inductive Bible Study

"But be doers of the word, and not hearers only, deceiving yourselves." James 1:22

Published By
Morningstar Christian Chapel
Whittier, California 90603

"True Faith Works"
James Inductive Bible Study
Copyright © 2001 by Morningstar Christian Chapel
Published by Morningstar Christian Chapel
ISBN: 978-1974647651
All rights reserved. No part of this book can be reproduced
in any form without written permission from the publisher.

Additional copies of this book are available by contacting:

Morningstar Christian Chapel
Whittier, California 90603
562.943.0297

Unless otherwise noted all Scripture quotations
are taken from the New King James Version,
Copyright © 1982 by Thomas Nelson, Inc.

Introduction

This letter was written to believers not unlike you and me. They, too, lived in a time of moral decay, political instability, and social deterioration. They experienced failure, disappointment, doubt, and major persecution for their faith, but they learned through the inspired teaching of this letter how these trials could be transformed into something eternally profitable.

James' hard-hitting, no-nonsense teaching exposed their carelessness, indifference and disobedience with love and compassion. His desire was to lead them into a deeper commitment to the Lord by showing them the necessity of doing—not just hearing—the Word of God. The same challenge is set before us through this study—**Will we be doers of the Word or just hearers only?**

"Faith without works," cannot be called faith. Faith must work, produce, and be visible. Verbal faith is not enough; mental faith is insufficient.

Faith endures trials and understands temptations. It will not allow us to consent to our lusts and slide into sin. Faith obeys the Word, producing doers of the Word. Faith harbors no prejudice. Faith and the respecting of persons cannot co-exist. Faith controls the tongue and follows after heavenly wisdom, turning its back on the wisdom of the world. Faith produces a separation from the world and enables us to "resist the devil" and humbly "draw near to God." Finally, faith waits patiently and steadfastly for the coming of the Lord for His church.

James and Paul do not contradict one another, but rather supplement each other. Paul teaches us to take the Gospel into our lives; James teaches us to live it out. Paul tells us the source of faith; James tells us the fruit of faith. Paul explains faith as the instrument by which a believer is justified before God; James explains that the faith which causes us to be "right-standing" with God will be evidenced by the way we live our lives. The same faith from different sides of the coin.

Background Information

AUTHOR:
Written by James, the brother of Jesus, the son of Mary and Joseph. James did not become a believer until he saw Jesus after the resurrection. He later became overseer of the church of Jerusalem. He was a respected leader and presided over the Council of Jerusalem recorded in Acts 15.

The historian, Eusebius, recorded the following description of James: **"James, the brother of the Lord, who, as there were many of this name, was surnamed 'the Just' by all, from the day of our Lord until now, received the government of the church with the apostles... He was in the habit of entering the temple alone, and was often found upon his bended knees, so that his knees became as hard as camels' knees."**

Tradition reports that James was martyred by stoning in 62 A.D. and that His final words were the same as those of our Lord, "Father, forgive them for they know not what they do."

WRITTEN TO:
In the days of the early church, the majority of which were Jewish believers, Christians were scattered throughout the world because of persecution. James writes to exhort and teach all those who were following Jesus Christ as Savior and Lord. Therefore, he is writing to exhort and encourage us to faithful living.

DATE OF WRITING:
Believed to be written before the famous council of Jerusalem in 49 A.D., which means it's probably the oldest of the twenty-seven books of the New Testament.

PURPOSE FOR WRITING:
The dominant theme of the book of James is faith that is real works practically in a person's life. James confronts his readers with the fact that Christianity must not only be believed; it must be lived.

KEYS TO JAMES:
Key Words: Faith that works
Key Verse: James 1:22

Study Outline

CHAPTER 1

The benefits of trials in God's hands: faith that trusts
An introduction . . . . vs. 1–2
Counting, knowing and letting God work . . . . vs. 3–5
By faith we receive wisdom . . . . vs. 6–8
The heavenly perspective . . . . vs. 9–11
Differentiating tests from temptations. . . . . vs. 12–18
Hearers, doers, and doers with a right heart! . . . . . vs. 19–27

CHAPTER 2

The benefits of faith in life and works
Delivering us from social partiality . . . . vs. 1–13
The work of faith is measurable. . . . . vs. 14–26

CHAPTER 3

The wisdom of faith in action and outlook
The untamable tongue tamed by the Lord . . . . vs. 1–12
The heavenly wisdom that rights our path . . . . vs. 13–18

CHAPTER 4

Faith challenges strife and presumption
Evil desires that rise from pride . . . . vs. 1–6
The humility that delivers us from worldliness . . . vs. 7–10
Evil speaking at its worst. vs. 11–12
Knowing today is all we can count on . . . . vs. 13–17

CHAPTER 5

Faith diversely applied
Sins of the rich. . . . . vs. 1–6
Examples of the prophets. vs. 7–12
Prayers that move mountains. . . . . vs. 13–18
Restoration. . . . . vs. 19–20

©2001—Morningstar Christian Chapel, Whittier, CA

Lesson Index

LESSON	TEXT	PAGE
1	James Overview	1
2	James 1:1–4	9
3	James 1:5–11	19
4	James 1:12–15	29
5	James 1:16–21	39
6	James 1:22–27	49
7	James 2:1–13	59
8	James 2:14–20	69
9	James 2:21–26	79
10	James 1–2 Review	89
11	James Review and Overview 3:1–4	99
12	James 3:5–12	109
13	James 3:13–18	119
14	James 4:1–6	129
15	James 4:7–10	139
16	James 4:11–17	151
17	James 5:1–6	161
18	James 5:7–12	171
19	James 5:13–20	181
20	James 1–5 Review	191

| OVERVIEW | 1 | LESSON #1 |

Remember to always begin every Bible Study in prayer. It is absolutely essential that we remember Who the Teacher is. We must call on the Holy Spirit to teach us and reveal the truth of God's Word to our hearts.

> Howbeit when He, the Spirit of truth, is come, He will guide you into all truth: for He shall not speak of Himself; but whatsoever He shall hear, that shall He speak: and He will shew you things to come. He shall glorify me: for He shall receive of mine, and shall shew it unto you. All things that the Father hath are mine: therefore said I, that He shall take of mine, and shall shew it unto you. John 16:13–15

DAY 1—BEGIN IN PRAYER

1. Read the Introductory pages of this study: **Introduction, Background Information, and Study Outline of James.**

2. Read the entire letter of James.
   (In one setting, without interruption, if possible.)

3. Record a few of the points that you found interesting or challenging.

   1 v 2-3 Count it all joy
   v6 - don't ask w/ doubt.
   v25 - effective doer - blessed in all he does.
   v27
   Chap 2 v 10
   B. v 17-18

4. Read the entire letter of James **again. (You can do it!)**

5. Is the letter of James more doctrinal or practical in it's teaching? Why?
   practical in its teaching because its hands on.
   It involves doing .... action ....

6. Write out James 1:22—this is considered the key verse of James. Begin to memorize this verse. *But prove yourselves doers of the word, and not merely hears who delude themselves*

DAY 2—BEGIN IN PRAYER

1. Read James chapter 1.

2. James writes from a very practical viewpoint. He is very direct and to the point—to follow his directions requires **action**. Record one thing you learn about each of the following subjects from chapter 1:

a. Temptations God does not temp. & cannot be tempted by evil — we are tempted when we give in to our desires & lust.

b. Wisdom — ask God for wisdom if you feel you are lacking it and He will give it to you, But ask in faith — do not doubt. or you will not receive.

c. Listening v 19 Be quick to hear, slow to speak & slow to anger.
Don't Just listen But put those words into action.

d. Pure Religion — If you think of yourself as religious & don't bridle your tongue (you deceive yourself) your religion is worthless. Pure & undefiled religion to God is to visit orphans & widows in need. & to keep oneself

3. We are exhorted to "be doers of the Word, not hearers only." What does James declare about the one who hears without action?

→ unstained by the world.

v 23-24 He is like a man who looks at his natural face in the mirror & once he looked & walked away he instantly forgets what kind of person he was.

4. What practical steps can we take, as believers, to keep ourselves "unspotted from the world"?

— put into practice what we read & learn → action
— don't give into our fleshly desires
— bridle our tongue
— ~~help others~~ treat others the way we want to be treated.

5. Is there an area that is addressed in chapter 1 that the Lord is specifically speaking to you about? Is there something you need to allow Him to change? Will you surrender it to Him in prayer today? Record your prayer here or in a personal journal. Share with the group, if you desire, the work He's doing in you.

be an effectual doer not just a doer.

DAY 3—BEGIN IN PRAYER

1. Read James chapter 2.

OVERVIEW 3 LESSON #1

2. What does James tell us about true faith and how it relates to others?

   True faith does not discriminate.

3. If we have "respect of persons," what are we doing? *judging*

   Love your neighbor as yourself.

4. What do we learn in chapter 2 about the **declaration** of faith that is not evidenced by the fruit of good works?

   faith w/out works is dead. — just as the body w/o the spirit is dead

5. Is there an area that is addressed in chapter 2 that the Lord is specifically speaking to you about? Is there something you need to allow Him to change? Will you surrender it to Him in prayer today? Record your prayer here or in a personal journal. Share with the group, if you desire, the work He's doing in you.

   do not judge — even in my thoughts
   repent & ask for forgiveness

DAY 4—BEGIN IN PRAYER

1. Read James chapter 3.

2. What one word would describe the subject of chapter 3:1-12? *(?)*

   Control? tongue?

3. How can this unruly member be tamed?

   Faith

4. Contrast the traits of wisdom **not** from above (**ungodly wisdom**) with wisdom from above (**godly wisdom**) from verses 13-18.

   Ungodly
   earthly, natural, demonic
   jealously, self ambition.
   disorder, & every evil thing.

   Godly
   pure, peaceable, gentle
   reasonable, full of mercy,
   good fruits, unwavering
   w/out hypocrisy.
   Seed is sown in peace
   by those who make
   peace.

   a. What is the end result of ungodly wisdom?

   3 v16 Where there is jealousy & self ambition, there is disorder & every evil thing.

b. What is the result of godly wisdom?

This wisdom is from above. Pure peaceable. ~ Seed whose fruit is Righteousness sown in peace by those who make peace

5. Is there an area that is addressed in chapter 3 that the Lord is specifically speaking to you about? Is there something you need to allow Him to change? Will you surrender it to Him in prayer today? Record your prayer here or in a personal journal. Share with the group, if you desire, the work He's doing in you.

Also my tone — Bridle my tongue more — not give in to worldly saying like I'm older I can say what I want.

It should be said in Love or Loving way not hurtful always

DAY 5 — BEGIN IN PRAYER

1. Read James chapter 4.

2. Record one detail you learned about each of the following topics from chapter 4:

   a. Internal warfare

   the source of our pleasures that wage war in us.

   b. Friendship with world is hostility toward God. If you wish to be friends w/ the world, you make an enemy w/ God

   c. Humility God is opposed to the proud, but give grace to the humble

   d. Future certainty He give a greater grace opposes the proud / grace to Humble
   Draw near to God & He will draw near to you
   Submit to God; Resist the devil & he will flee from you

3. God promises to respond to our steps of faith. From the following verses, list our responsibility and then God's faithful response to our obedience:

	OUR RESPONSIBILITY	GOD'S RESPONSE
a. Verse 7	Submit to God. Resist the devil	the devil will flee
b. Verse 8a	Draw near to God	He will draw near to me.
c. Verse 10	Humble myself in the presence of the Lord	He will lift me up / exalt me.

4. Record the very clear declaration in verse 17 and tell how this truth affects the choices and decisions that we make every day. the one who know the right thing to do + does not do it, to him it is sin. When we are tempted in day to day living we must choose the right thing + be a witness to the world

5. Is there an area that is addressed in chapter 4 that the Lord is specifically speaking to you about? Is there something you need to allow Him to change? Will you surrender it to Him in prayer today? Record your prayer here or in a personal journal. Share with the group, if you desire, the work He's doing in you. Don't forget to ask.

DAY 6—BEGIN IN PRAYER

1. Read James chapter 5.

2. What severe warning do you find in this chapter to those who mistreat, misuse and persecute the brethren?
They will be judged harshly.

3. What are we to do, as believers, so that we can steadfastly endure hardship and unfair treatment? **How are you doing?**

   Be patient don't complain, endure. Do not swear. Let your yes be yes + your no be no — so you will not fall under judgement.

4. As James closes his letter, he deals with the tremendous power of prayer that is the result of true faith. Record a few details about prayer from verses 13-18.

   Suffering — pray
   Cheerful — sing praises
   Sick — elders anoint oil
   Confess sins to one another
   Effective prayer of a Righteous man can accomplish much.

5. Is there an area that is addressed in chapter 5 that the Lord is specifically speaking to you about? Is there something you need to allow Him to change? Will you surrender it to Him in prayer today? Record your prayer here or in a personal journal. Share with the group, if you desire, the work He's doing in you.

   Prayer for being more outspoken in prayer / Groups.
   — Pray —

Optional Assignment: Compare the parallels of James' teaching with the teaching of Christ on the Sermon on the Mount.

James 1:22   Matthew 7:24

James 3:12   Matthew 7:16

OVERVIEW   **LESSON #1**

James 4:11, 12   Matthew 7:1

James 5:2   Matthew 6:19

James 5:12   Matthew 5:34–37

Search me, O God, and know my heart: try me, and know my thoughts: And see if there be any wicked way in me, and lead me in the way everlasting. Psalms 139:23, 24

8

JAMES 1:1–4 — LESSON #2

DAY 1—BEGIN IN PRAYER (This is the most important part of the study!)

1. Read James 1:1–4.

2. There are several men named James who are mentioned in the New Testament. However, it is commonly believed that the writer of this letter is James, the half-brother of Jesus, the son of Mary and Joseph. What do we learn about the writer, James, from the following Scripture references?

   ? a. John 7:1–5   he did not believe in Jesus

   b. 1 Corinthians 15:1–7   Jesus appeared to James after His ressurection

   c. Acts 1:14   He believed!! — devoting to prayer.

3. James became a prominent leader in the early church. He was the pastor of the church of Jerusalem and played an important role in the development of the church. What more do we learn about James from these references?

   a. Acts 12:16, 17 — Peter told them to report to James how the Lord freed them from jail

   b. Acts 15:13–20 (If you are not familiar with this meeting, read verses 1–30.) He told the other to write the gentiles who has turned to faith + tell them to abstain from idols fornication + from what is strangled + from blood.

   c. Acts 21:17–19   Paul told James (an elder) and the other elders what God had done among the gentiles thru his (Paul) ministry

JAMES 1:1-4 — LESSON #2

    d. Galatians 1:15-19

Paul met ~~Cephas~~ w/ ~~James~~ Cephas & also saw James

    e. Galatians 2:7-10

He ministered to the gentiles w/ Paul, John, & Cephas.

4. To whom was this letter written?

? Paul ~~also~~ wrote it to the Galatians (the Church?) Jerusalem

Why were they scattered abroad? Acts 8:1

a great persecution arose against the church in Jerusalem scattered in Judea & Samaria except the apostles.

What was the results of their being forced out of Jerusalem? Acts 11:19-21

Some spoke only to Jews. But some began to speak to the greek & the the LORD blessed & many believed.

Pagan worship was the norm throughout the Roman Empire in the first century. Can you imagine yourself as a believer who was **scattered** abroad in these unfamiliar countries? What difficulties might you face?

Death, persecution or succumbing to their pagan gods

5. How does the Bible describe the life of the believer in this world?

    a. 1 Chronicles 29:15 *we are sojourners before Thee, tenants on the earth*

    b. Psalms 119:19; 54 *I am a stranger on the earth*

Thy statutes are my songs in the house of my pilgrimage

c. Hebrews 11:13-16

exiles from earth, (seeking a country of) v-14 ??
A better country - a heavenly one (their own)
God has prepare a city for us.

d. 1Peter 2:11, 12

Aliens + strangers
Keep your behavior excellent among the non believers.

Personal: Do you sometimes feel that you are "scattered abroad"? How are you doing being an effective pilgrim? Are you holding too tightly to the stuff of this world? *No. Not holding tightly to worldly things (At least I don't think so) — I feel scattered yes. many times*

6. Use James 1:2-4 as your memory verse this week. Record it here and begin working on it today. (**Write it out on a 3x5 card and carry it with you.**)

Consider it all joy when you encounter various trials. Knowing that the testing of your faith produces endurance. + let the endurance have its perfect result, that you may be perfect + complete, lacking in nothing.

DAY 2—BEGIN IN PRAYER

1. Read James 1:1-4.

2. Re-read James 1:1.

3. James introduces himself as a **servant**. In his culture, and ours, it would not be uncommon for a man of his qualifications to boast in his lineage and accomplishments. James was content to be known as a **servant** of God and of the Lord Jesus Christ. Use a Dictionary of New Testament Words, a Strong's Concordance, or an English Language Dictionary to give you a deeper meaning of this word **servant**.

4. The word **servant** (doulos = Greek) denotes one who **is deprived of his personal freedom and so becomes fully an instrument in the hands of his master.** He is the one who can never say "no" to his master. It implies a willing commitment to be bound together for life. What do we learn about this bond-slave commitment from the following Scriptures?

a. Matthew 16:24, 25

b. John 15:18-21

c. 1Corinthians 6:19, 20

d. Colossians 3:1-4

5. What difference would it make in our lifestyle if we truly considered ourselves as bond-slaves of our Lord?

Do you think a bond-servant of a righteous master is concerned about what they will do, where they will live, or what they are to eat, drink, and wear? These are the concerns of the master. How much more rest ought we, who are the servants of God and the Lord Jesus Christ, to experience! Read and meditate on the following passages of Scripture. What do they say to you?

a. Matthew 6:19-21

b. Matthew 6:25-34

6. Is there an area of your life that the Lord is specifically speaking to you about today? Is there something you need to allow Him to change? Will you surrender it to Him in prayer today? Record your prayer here or in a personal journal.

JAMES 1:1–4 — LESSON #2

DAY 3—BEGIN IN PRAYER

1. Read James 1:1–4.

2. Re-read James 1:2.

3. Use a Dictionary of New Testament Words to find the more accurate meaning of the following KJV words:

   a. Count

   b. Fall

   c. Divers

   d. Temptations

   Use a different translation and record verse 2 below.

4. James lovingly instructs us about how we ought to—and need to—face the trying of our faith that is sure to come. As believers, we are not to divide our lives into pleasant or unpleasant, good or bad. We are to face the trying of our faith and **count** (**hegeomai = consider; deem; account; think**) it good because it is the tool by which we will grow in spiritual maturity. What more do we learn about these tests of our faith?

   a. Deuteronomy 8:1–3

JAMES 1:1-4   14   LESSON #2

    b. Romans 5:3-5

    c. 1Peter 1:6, 7

    d. 1Peter 4:12, 13

5. Take notice that this verse says "**when** you fall into temptation." There is no question of **if**, it **will** happen daily. This verse is speaking of temptations or tests that come from the outside (in verse 14 James will discuss the internal temptations). There are temptations from the world, those which we have no control over, that we are thrown into by virtue of our daily experience. These temptations the enemy uses hoping to cause us to fall. However, God uses them as tools to strengthen our faith. What is to be our reaction when we face these trials that come in many different forms, from every different direction?

    a. 2Chronicles 33:11-13

    b. Matthew 4:3-11

    c. Ephesians 6:11-13

    d. James 4:7, 8

6. Is there an area of your life that the Lord is specifically speaking to you about today? Is there something you need to allow Him to change? Will you surrender it to Him in prayer today? Record your prayer here or in a personal journal.

JAMES 1:1–4	LESSON #2

DAY 4—BEGIN IN PRAYER

1. Read James 1:1–4.

2. Re-read James 1:3.

3. Use your dictionary to define the following words to help you get a better grasp of their meaning:

   a. Knowing

   b. Trying

   c. Faith

   d. Patience

4. Define faith as described in Hebrews 11:1–3.

   What things were wrought by faith in Hebrews 11:33, 34?

5. James gives us the reason that we can "count it all joy." We need to have an eternal outlook seeing the purpose that God has in store for us. **Knowing (ginosko = recognize; understand; learn; perceive)** that the "trying of your faith produces patience." Record the truths that you discover about patience.

   a. Romans 2:6, 7

JAMES 1:1-4 — LESSON #2

    b. Romans 15:4-6

    c. Hebrews 10:35-37

    d. Hebrews 12:1, 2

6. Is there an area of your life that the Lord is specifically speaking to you about today? Is there something you need to allow Him to change? Will you surrender it to Him in prayer today? Record your prayer here or in a personal journal.

DAY 5—BEGIN IN PRAYER

1. Read James 1:1-4. **(Don't skip this part!)**

2. Re-read James 1:4.

3. According to this verse, what is the end result of our enduring under the trials in our lives?

    What word in this verse indicates that we have a choice about facing trials? How does that choice affect the outcome?

4. James teaches us that when we stand steadfast under trials with our eyes on the Lord, knowing that He has a perfect plan for us, we will become mature in faith and strong in character. In order to trust Him with our lives, we must be confident about Who He is, how much He loves us, and what He plans for us. Record and meditate on the following passages of Scripture asking the Lord to increase your faith in Him.

©2001—MORNINGSTAR CHRISTIAN CHAPEL, WHITTIER, CA

JAMES 1:1–4   17   LESSON #2

    a. Deuteronomy 7:7–9

    b. Jeremiah 29:11–13

    c. Romans 8:28–31

    d. Romans 8:35–39

5. Record Job's perspective on the end product of the trial of his faith from Job 23:10.

Personal: Can you testify with the same confidence about your life? It is a matter of choice. Will you persevere in trials or fight against them?

6. Is there an area of your life that the Lord is specifically speaking to you about today? Is there something you need to allow Him to change? Will you surrender it to Him in prayer today? Record your prayer here or in a personal journal.

DAY 6—BEGIN IN PRAYER

1. Read James 1:1–4.

2. What one or two things do you understand differently about these verses as they apply to your life?

3. Can you share a specific situation where trials have made you more patient and more mature?

4. Have you memorized James 1:2-4? Keep working on it, it is the key to spiritual growth.

> My brethren, count it all joy when ye fall into divers temptations;
> James 1:2

JAMES 1:5-11 — LESSON #3

DAY 1—BEGIN IN PRAYER

1. Read James 1:5-11.

2. Read James 1:2-4. According to the context of this chapter, what is the reason we must ask God for wisdom?

3. Why should the believer of "low degree rejoice" and the brother who is "rich in this world" walk in humility? How should this truth affect our view of the Body of believers?

4. Choose a verse to memorize this week. Begin working on it today.

DAY 2—BEGIN IN PRAYER

1. Read James 1:5-11.

2. Re-read James 1:5, 6.

3. The most important thing we can realize when facing the testing of our faith is that we cannot make it on our own. Not in our own power, our own strength or our own wisdom. We need to first recognize our inability and **ask**! What warning is recorded to those who think themselves wise? What reminder is there to us to ask, in humility, for God to give us His wisdom?

    a. Proverbs 3:5-7

    b. Proverbs 26:12

©2001—Morningstar Christian Chapel, Whittier, CA

JAMES 1:5-11   20   LESSON #3

   c. Luke 18:9-14

   d. Revelation 3:15-19

4. James speaks of the manner in which God gives His wisdom which is so necessary in our lives. The adverb used here is **haploos** in Greek. It is translated in King James **liberally** but also means: **to spread out; stretch forth.** James wants to teach us that we have a God whose hand is stretched forth, whose bounties are spread out before us, and who has an abundant provision of wisdom waiting for those who will ask. There is no shame in the fact that we lack. What more can we learn about our Father who is waiting for us to call upon His Name?

   a. Psalm 34:8-10

   b. Luke 11:9-13

   c. John 15:7

   d. Hebrews 4:16

5. Now we know that we need wisdom and we know that we need to ask God for it; but there is a condition we need to meet in order to receive wisdom in our trials. What is it?

| JAMES 1:5–11 | LESSON #3 |

When we ask for wisdom and do not receive, we should not come to the conclusion that God is slack in His promises. The fault lies in our asking. When we believe God, we must believe that He is absolute and is able to do that which may not be within the range of our experience or reasoning. What does God's Word teach us about faith and our relationship to the Father?

    a. Mark 11:22–24

    b. Hebrews 10:23

    c. Hebrews 11:1–3

    d. Hebrews 11:6

6. Is there an area of your life that the Lord is specifically speaking to you about today? Is there something you need to allow Him to change? Will you surrender it to Him in prayer today? Record your prayer here or in a personal journal.

DAY 3—BEGIN IN PRAYER

1. Read James 1:5–11.

2. Re-read James 1:7–8.

3. Since we are to "ask in faith," Who or what are we to base our faith on? When we doubt, Whose ability are we doubting? What do we learn about our Heavenly Father that will encourage and strengthen our faithful petition for wisdom?

a. Jeremiah 10:10-13

b. Jeremiah 32:17-19

c. Matthew 19:26

d. Luke 1:37

4. If we ask God for wisdom in the midst of a trial but doubt that He will supply it, or doubt that we need His help, what will we get from the Lord?

From the following examples, what can we determine must be our heart's cry when we come to our Lord in prayer?

a. Psalm 40:8

b. Matthew 6:9, 10

c. Luke 22:41, 42

d. John 4:34

JAMES 1:5–11   LESSON #3

5. In verse 8, James gives us a vivid picture of the one who does not ask in faith. "He is a double-minded man, unstable in all his ways." He is literally a "two-souled" man. He has one soul that believes and one that does not. John Bunyan called him, "Mr. Facing-both-ways." Contrast this double-minded man with the trusting one of Proverbs 3:5–8.

   What phrase is repeated in both Scriptures?

   What is the obvious opposite result of whole-heartedly trusting God?

   Personal: How are you doing? Are you stable or unstable?

6. Is there an area of your life that the Lord is specifically speaking to you about today? Is there something you need to allow Him to change? Will you surrender it to Him in prayer today? Record your prayer here or in a personal journal.

DAY 4—BEGIN IN PRAYER

1. Read James 1:5–11.

2. Re-read James 1:9.

3. Why does the believer who is of **low degree (of humble circumstances; low in rank; poor; powerless)** have a reason to rejoice?

JAMES 1:5–11   24   LESSON #3

Record the abundant, true wealth of the believer:

a. 2Corinthians 4:6, 7

b. Ephesians 2:11–13

c. 1Peter 1:3–5

d. 1John 3:2, 3

4. Who is it that has exalted us? What do we learn from the following references about the character of the person whom the Lord lifts up?

a. Isaiah 66:2

b. Matthew 18:3–5

c. Matthew 23:12

d. 1Peter 5:5, 6

JAMES 1:5–11 — LESSON #3

5. What directions and warnings do we find in these Scriptures regarding the temptation to envy and covet and the need to be content?

   a. Matthew 6:19–21

   b. Colossians 3:1, 2

   c. 1 Timothy 6:6–10

   d. Hebrews 13:5

6. Is there an area of your life that the Lord is specifically speaking to you about today? Is there something you need to allow Him to change? Will you surrender it to Him in prayer today? Record your prayer here or in a personal journal.

DAY 5—BEGIN IN PRAYER (Remember it is the Holy Spirit that teaches us!)

1. Read James 1:5–11.

2. Re-read James 1:10, 11.

3. In contrast to verse 9, how is the believer who is rich in this world's goods made humble?

JAMES 1:5–11   LESSON #3

The contrast of poverty and wealth draws our attention to the divers temptations or various trials we could fall into in either circumstance. Often the poor man thinks his problems are far worse than the rich man's, but the perils of prosperity can be just as dangerous. What instruction do we find in God's Word regarding the riches of this world?

a. Deuteronomy 8:11–17

b. Jeremiah 9:23, 24

c. Psalm 62:10

d. 1 Timothy 6:17–19

4. Record Proverbs 23:4, 5 below and ask the Lord to protect your heart against setting your affection on those things that do not last!

5. James closes this paradox with an illustration that drives home the truth by giving us a picture of the hot desert sun. No sooner does it rise above the horizon than the plants begin to wither and die; the blossoms fall and its beauty fades. In the same way, the rich man's wealth is fading away even as he goes about his business. In Philippians 4:11, 12, what does Paul teach us to do so we are not stumbled by the lack of, or the abundance of, material wealth?

JAMES 1:5-11 — LESSON #3

Personal: Ask the Lord to help you learn to be content by listing all the blessings you have been given.

6. Is there an area of your life that the Lord is specifically speaking to you about today? Is there something you need to allow Him to change? Will you surrender it to Him in prayer today? Record your prayer here or in a personal journal.

DAY 6—BEGIN IN PRAYER

1. Read James 1:5-11.

2. Practice making it a habit in your prayer life to ask God for wisdom daily to face the divers temptations that will come your way. What do you need wisdom for today?

3. When you ask, will God give wisdom? How?

4. What is the result of this prayer if you doubt that He will answer or you doubt that you need His wisdom?

5. What is the lifestyle description of this doubting one?

6. Ask the Lord to give you a clear view of His ability to keep you in the midst of, and lead you through, the temptations you face.

If any of you lack wisdom, let him ask of God, that giveth to all men liberally, and upbraideth not; and it shall be given him. James 1:5

JAMES 1:12-15   LESSON #4

DAY 1—BEGIN IN PRAYER

1. Read James 1:12-15.

2. Look up the definitions of the following words in a concordance or an expository dictionary so that you have a deeper understanding of their meaning.

   a. Endures (v.12)

   b. Tried (v.12)

   c. Drawn Away (v.14)

   d. Lust (v.14)

   e. Sin (v.15)

3. What do we learn from Psalm 119:133 that will keep us from being dominated by the power of sin?

4. Choose a verse(s) to memorize this week. **(May I suggest James 1:13-15.)** Begin working on it today.

©2001—MORNINGSTAR CHRISTIAN CHAPEL, WHITTIER, CA

JAMES 1:12–15 — LESSON #4

DAY 2—BEGIN IN PRAYER

1. Read James 1:12–15.

2. Re-read James 1:12.

3. In this verse we are given an awesome incentive for perseverance and a guaranteed promise to those who love Him. The rewards of the testing of our faith are both present and future. The man who endures the trying of his faith will see fruit now and in eternity. What more do we learn about the present and future outcome of victorious endurance through testing?

    a. Mark 10:29, 30

    b. Romans 8:16–18

    c. 1 Peter 1:6–9

    d. James 1:2–4

4. According to James 1:12 the blessed person is the one who **endures**. What does the word **endure** signify to you?

    What do the following Scriptures teach us about **endurance**?

    a. Matthew 24:9–13

b. 2Timothy 2:3-5

c. Hebrews 11:24-27

d. Hebrews 12:1-4

5. The term "crown of life" is used symbolically here meaning: **eternal life with the Lord**. What is the motivating factor that causes the believer to endure or persevere under trials?

What will be the obvious outward proof in your daily life that you will be receiving the "crown of life"?

a. John 14:15

b. John 14:21

c. John 15:10-12

d. 1John 2:3-6

6. Is there an area of your life that the Lord is specifically speaking to you about today? Is there something you need to allow Him to change? Will you surrender it to Him in prayer today? Record your prayer here or in a personal journal.

DAY 3—BEGIN IN PRAYER

1. Read James 1:12–15.

2. Re-read James 1:13.

3. In verses 13–15, James used the same basic Greek word for **tempted** that he used for **trials** in verses 2 and 12. But this time he moves from the noun, **peirasmos**, to the verb, **peirazo**. When he does this, it seems that he changes the use of **peiramos** from **external trials** or **testing** (vs. 2; 12) to **inward temptations** or **solicitations to do evil** (vs. 13–17). What is the natural tendency of man when faced with sin?

Blaming began very early in the history of mankind. Record the details of the first recorded blame-shifting incident from Genesis 3:11–13. **Have you been guilty of this common practice of sin today?**

Why should we never blame God for our personal failures? Psalm 145:17.

4. We must **never** say, or even imagine, that God is tempting us. He **never** has and He **never** will. What do the following Scriptures teach us about the character of God and how do they remind you that God **cannot** tempt you to evil?

   a. Leviticus 11:45

| JAMES 1:12–15 | LESSON #4 |

b. Deuteronomy 32:4

c. Revelation 15:3, 4

5. It is important we see that we have the responsibility to **choose** how we react to every circumstance in our lives. A particular circumstance that God allows to **test** our faith **(approve; reveal)** may be turned into a **temptation to sin** depending on how we react to that circumstance. We have been given a promise of escape and all the needed provision to do so. What powerful reminders do we find in these promises?

a. 1Corinthians 10:13

b. Ephesians 6:12, 13

c. Philippians 2:13

6. Is there an area of your life that the Lord is specifically speaking to you about today? Is there something you need to allow Him to change? Will you surrender it to Him in prayer today? Record your prayer here or in a personal journal.

DAY 4—BEGIN IN PRAYER

1. Read James 1:12–15.

JAMES 1:12–15   LESSON #4

2. Re-read James 1:14.

3. Having made a powerful defense of the character of God, James now tells us the **source** of temptation in no uncertain words. He points to the source of the temptation as being our own evil nature. **Lust** refers to **evil desire**. What does God's Word teach us about the natural state of man's heart.

   a. Jeremiah 17:9

   b. Psalms 53:1–3

   c. Proverbs 28:26

   d. Ecclesiastes 9:3

4. The illustration that James uses is the picture of a fisherman baiting a hook to catch a fish. The same process takes place when we are tempted by our own **illicit desires (lusts)**. When temptation passes by, we are **drawn away** from the things that keep us safe. Soon they are far behind us as we are **lured** by the bright, delicious temptation and in a moment we forget who we are and throw caution to the wind…and bite. Hooked! Sin! What do we learn from the following Scriptures that keeps us from being hooked by the lure of sin?

   a. Matthew 4:1–11

JAMES 1:12–15   35   LESSON #4

    b. Galatians 5:16

    c. Colossians 3:1–3

    d. James 4:7–10

5. Let's look back at the trials of James 1:2–12. When we go through trials and do not "count it all joy," what are our alternative reactions? List them.

Personal: Can you see when the trial allowed for testing and maturing your faith becomes a temptation to sin? How will this truth help you today?

6. Is there an area of your life that the Lord is specifically speaking to you about today? Is there something you need to allow Him to change? Will you surrender it to Him in prayer today? Record your prayer here or in a personal journal.

DAY 5—BEGIN IN PRAYER

1. Read James 1:12–15.

2. Read James 1:15.

JAMES 1:12–15   LESSON #4

3. Record the sequence and final consequence of yielding to the lust of our hearts.

   a.

   b.

   c.

4. Use the progression of Eve's sin in Genesis 3 to illustrate this truth. Record the Scriptures to support your answers.

5. James changes the illustration to the familiar terminology of childbirth. However, the end result of this birth is not what we expect. Sin looks tempting, pleasurable, and exciting, but when it is brought to full-term it is not alive—it brings forth death. Record what John tells us about those things that bring death and our responsibility toward them.

   a. 1John 2:15–17

Every temptation requires a decision on our part. We must decide rather to choose to walk in obedience to the Lord or according to the lust of our flesh. Record Galatians 6:7–9 and use it as a reminder to walk in obedience today.

JAMES 1:12-15 — LESSON #4

6. Is there an area of your life that the Lord is specifically speaking to you about today? Is there something you need to allow Him to change? Will you surrender it to Him in prayer today? Record your prayer here or in a personal journal.

DAY 6—BEGIN IN PRAYER

1. Read James 1:12-15.

2. What have you learned this week that has helped you to **endure** temptation?

3. Do you have a different perspective on temptation and its source than you did at the beginning of the week? Explain.

4. Knowing that God does **not** tempt you to sin, whose responsibility is it to make right choices? **How are you doing?**

5. Have you completed your memory verse? If not, do so today.

> Blessed is the man that endureth temptation: for when he is tried, he shall receive the crown of life, which the Lord hath promised to them that love him. James 1:12

38

JAMES 1:16–21 — LESSON #5

DAY 1 — BEGIN IN PRAYER

1. Read James 1:16–21.

2. We find a paragraph division in this week's study. Record the contents of each part with a short sentence.

    a. James 1:16–18

    b. James 1:19–21

3. Use a Dictionary of New Testament Words, Strong's Concordance or an English Language Dictionary to find further meanings for the following words:

    a. Err (v. 16)

    b. Variableness (v. 17)

    c. Receive (v. 21)

    d. Engrafted (v. 21)

4. Choose a verse to memorize this week. Begin working on it today.

JAMES 1:16–21 — LESSON #5

DAY 2—BEGIN IN PRAYER

1. Read James 1:16–21.

2. Re-read James 1:16.

3. What warning is given to us in this connecting verse? (**Note: to whom it is written.**)

   Using the context of these verses, in what way might we **err** in our thoughts or actions?

4. James cautions us to keep from being deceived and straying from the truth. Under what circumstances or by whose influence **could** we be deceived? Formulate your answer from the following Scriptures references.

   a. Matthew 22:29

   b. 2Corinthians 11:3

   c. Ephesians 4:14

   d. Colossians 2:4

5. As believers, we have been given every necessary tool and the ability to keep from **erring**, record just a few and begin to **fervently** practice using them today?

a. 1Corinthians 2:12, 13

b. Ephesians 6:11–13

c. 2Timothy 3:16, 17

d. Hebrews 4:15, 16

6. Is there an area of your life that the Lord is specifically speaking to you about today? Is there something you need to allow Him to change? Will you surrender it to Him in prayer today? Record your prayer here or in a personal journal.

Day 3—Begin in Prayer

1. Read James 1:16–21.

2. Re-read James 1:17, 18.

3. After James clearly teaches us that God is **not** responsible for, or involved in, the temptation of man to do evil, he turns to the positive side revealing the true nature of God. He is good, therefore He gives only good gifts and their purpose is to accomplish good things in our lives. What does God's Word tell us about these gifts and their Giver?

a. Isaiah 55:8–11

JAMES 1:16-21 — LESSON #5

    b. Jeremiah 29:11

    c. Matthew 7:9-11

    d. Romans 8:28

4. Our Heavenly Father is good, His gifts are good and perfect, and they will produce His desired work in our lives. It was true when James wrote this letter and it is true today. He is Light, the Creator of the heavenly lights, and the Giver of all good things—He doesn't change. How do the following verses help you when you face trials that do not have an **obvious** good purpose?

    a. Psalm 103:17

    b. Isaiah 44:6

    c. Malachi 3:6

    d. Hebrews 13:8

5. Because every gift is good and the method and reason for giving is good, James gives us the perfect example of God's goodness. It is according to His **will** (His **desire**) that we can be born again by the Word of Truth. Observe and record the truth of the goodness of the gifts of God.

a. John 3:16, 17

b. Romans 6:23

c. Ephesians 2:8, 9

d. 1John 4:9, 10
Do not err in taking His awesome gifts for granted!

6. Is there an area of your life that the Lord is specifically speaking to you about today? Is there something you need to allow Him to change? Will you surrender it to Him in prayer today? Record your prayer here or in a personal journal.

DAY 4—BEGIN IN PRAYER

1. Read James 1:16–21.

2. Re-read James 1:19, 20.

3. Verse 19 begins with "wherefore," referring back to the truths that James has just stated: only good comes from God. The Gift-giver is the good Father of creation, His goodness will never change, and His goodness is exemplified in our salvation. **Wherefore,** we have a three-part responsibility. What is it?

    1.

2.

3.

4. In context, this exhortation refers primarily to our hearing God and listening to Him and His Word. When thinking in terms of listening to God, why is it necessary that we be:

Quick to hear?

a. Romans 10:17

b. Hebrews 4:12

Slow to speak?

a. Ecclesiastes 5:1, 2

b. Matthew 12:36, 37

Slow to wrath?

a. Proverbs 18:12

b. 1 Peter 5:5

JAMES 1:16–21   LESSON #5

Extra Credit Challenge: This exhortation also effectively applies to our relationships with one another. Explain how doing this would improve the health of the Body of Christ or even your family.

5. A very important truth is revealed to us in verse 20. It may be something we already know, however, we seem to forget it in an instant when we get angry. What other insight do we gain from these Scriptures that remind us that we cannot accomplish God's work through our flesh?

   a. Numbers 20:11, 12

   b. Galatians 3:3

   c. 2Timothy 2:24, 25

   d. James 3:17, 18

6. Is there an area of your life that the Lord is specifically speaking to you about today? Is there something you need to allow Him to change? Will you surrender it to Him in prayer today? Record your prayer here or in a personal journal.

Day 5—Begin in Prayer

1. Read James 1:16–21.

2. Re-read James 1:21.

JAMES 1:16-21 — LESSON #5

3. We are instructed to "lay apart **(lay aside; put off)** all filthiness." The word translated **filthiness (rhuparia)** is not used anywhere else in the New Testament. In classical Greek it carries the idea of **wax in ears** referring to evil conduct specifically described as an unwillingness to listen, a sinful tongue, and unrighteous anger. We are to lay aside sin because it keeps us from receiving the Word of God. What are some of these specific sins as recorded in the Scripture?

   a. Ephesians 4:25-31

   b. Colossians 3:5-9

   Personal: How will continuing to hold on and practice these sins hinder your reception or acceptance of the Word? Is there a specific sin that you continue to hold on to that keeps you from having fertile soil in your heart to receive the truth of the Word?

4. If we are to receive with meekness the engrafted Word, what is required in the heart of the believer?

   a. Isaiah 57:15

   b. Micah 6:8

   c. Matthew 23:11, 12

JAMES 1:16–21 — LESSON #5

    d. James 4:8–10

5. What provides ideal soil for the implanted Word and how will the following verses help prepare the soil?

    a. 1John 1:9

    b. Psalm 51:1–4

    c. Jeremiah 4:3

    d. Hosea 10:12

Challenge: What parallels can you draw from Jesus' Parable of the Sower (Matthew 13:3–9) and James 1:21b?

6. Is there an area of your life that the Lord is specifically speaking to you about today? Is there something you need to allow Him to change? Will you surrender it to Him in prayer today? Record your prayer here or in a personal journal.

JAMES 1:16–21   **LESSON #5**

DAY 6—BEGIN IN PRAYER

1. Read James 1:16–21.

2. Did the lesson this week reveal any area in which you have erred in your thinking or action? Ask the Lord to make this revelation a permanent change in your life.

2. Explain how James 1:17, 18 encourages you when you are experiencing temptation to sin?

3. Have you taken notice of how **quick** to hear, how **slow** to speak, how **slow** to wrath you have been this week? Is there room for improvement? Ask the Lord specifically to help you in one area.

4. If a person chooses to disregard James 1:21, what might be the result in his orher life?

5. Did you complete you memory verse this week. **If not, do so today.**

> Thy words were found, and I did eat them; and thy word was unto me the joy and rejoicing of mine heart: for I am called by thy name, O LORD God of hosts. Jeremiah 15:16

> Wherefore, my beloved brethren, let every man be swift to hear, slow to speak, slow to wrath: James 1:19

JAMES 1:22-27   LESSON #6

DAY 1—BEGIN IN PRAYER

1. Read James 1:22-27.

2. Use your Dictionary of New Testament Words, Strong's Concordance or English Language Dictionary to find a deeper meaning of the following words:

   a. Doer (v. 22)

   b. Beholding (v. 23)

   c. Looks (v. 25)

   d. Continues (v. 25)

3. With the help of the above definitions answer the following questions:

   a. What is the outcome in the life of the one who is a **hearer** of the Word?

   b. Do you think the **hearer** of the Word **understands** what he hears?

   c. What **may** be some reasons he does not become a **doer**?

d. What seems to be different in the life of the one who is described in verse 25?

e. What is the outcome of being a **doer** of the work?

f. What are three external proofs of the validity of a pure relationship with God the Father found in verses 26 and 27?

4. James is giving us a strong warning of the need for every believer to **apply** God's Word to his or her life. Doing the study each week is not enough. We must **live** what we are learning. Be sure to make it your prayer this week to allow the Lord to cause you to be a faithful **doer** of the Word. Memorize James 1:22 this week and make it your daily prayer.

Day 2—Begin in Prayer

1. Read James 1:22–27.

2. Re-read James 1:22. **(How are you doing at memorizing it? Better yet doing it?)**

3. Can you imagine hearing Jesus speaking directly to you as those on the Mount of Beatitudes did? Record His instructions from the following verses and consider them in relationship to your being a **doer** of the Word.

    a. Matthew 5:16

    b. Matthew 5:44

JAMES 1:22–27   51   LESSON #6

    c. Matthew 6:19–21

    d. Matthew 6:31–33

    e. Matthew 7:7, 8

    f. Matthew 7:12

4. What warnings and truths do we find in the Scriptures about this temptation to be **hearers**?

    a. Matthew 7:21–27

    b. Romans 2:13

    c. James 4:17

5. The word **deceiving** means to **reckon falsely; miscalculate; delude.** If we think we are doing righteously because we faithfully attend services, faithfully study the Bible and faithfully receive the teaching of the Scriptures, but we are not allowing them freedom to change the way we live

JAMES 1:22–27 — **LESSON #6**

we deceive ourselves. What is the true proof in the life of a believer that the Word of God has penetrated the heart?

a. John 14:23

b. 1Peter 1:22, 23

c. 1John 2:5, 6

d. 1John 3:24

Personal: What do you know to do and are not doing? Confess and repent and the Lord will enable you to be obedient to His Word.

6. Is there an area of your life that the Lord is specifically speaking to you about today? Is there something you need to allow Him to change? Will you surrender it to Him in prayer today? Record your prayer here or in a personal journal.

Day 3—Begin in Prayer

1. Read James 1:22–27.

2. Re-read James 1:23, 24.

3. James gives us a vivid illustration of this man who is a **hearer** only. He likens him to a man who takes a good, attentive, understanding look at his natural face in a mirror and seeing the truth of who he is, he immediately goes away and forgets what manner of man he is. Read the Words of the Lord to Ezekiel the Prophet in Ezekiel 33:30–32. Describe the heart of the people.

JAMES 1:22–27   53   LESSON #6

Were these people **hearers of the Word?**

Record God's judgment of their disobedient lives from Ezekiel 33:23–29.

4. Verse 24 says this man **beholds (looks intently at)** himself in a mirror (looking-glass). This mirror is a symbolic description of the Word of God. What effect does the Word of God have on our lives as believers?

   a. Jeremiah 23:29

   b. John 15:3

   c. Ephesians 5:25b–27

   d. 1 Thessalonians 2:13

   e. Hebrews 4:12, 13

5. Intently looking into the mirror of the Word of God not only gives us an accurate reflection of our need for a Savior, it also reflects the holiness of God. This reflection causes us either to repent or to run away trying to forget what we have seen. What was the reaction of these men of the Bible when they came face-to-face with the true and living Holy God?

   a. Isaiah 6:5

b. Job 42:5, 6

c. Luke 5:8

Personal: Is this the attitude of your heart as you approach the Lord through His Word?

6. Is there an area of your life that the Lord is specifically speaking to you about today? Is there something you need to allow Him to change? Will you surrender it to Him in prayer today? Record your prayer here or in a personal journal.

DAY 4—BEGIN IN PRAYER (Don't forget Who the teacher is!)

1. Read James 1:22–27.

2. Re-read James 1:25.

3. Turning from the folly of the first man, James now directs us to the wisdom of the second. This man looks intently "into the perfect law of liberty." He finds freedom from the bondage of sin, freedom to surrender to his Lord and Savior, and freedom to worship and obey. What further details do we learn about our freedom in Christ?

    a. John 8:31, 32

    b. Romans 8:1, 2

JAMES 1:22–27   55   LESSON #6

   c. 2 Corinthians 3:17, 18

   d. Galatians 5:13

4. Notice that James tells us this second man, the **doer** of the work, **continues (to remain beside, continue always near)** in the Word. He lives in profound obedience. He keeps looking and doing; looking and doing; looking and doing. He has become part of a God-created process in which knowledge followed by obedience brings more knowledge. Read the **Parable of the Talents** in Matthew 25:14–29. How does this illustrate our need to act upon what we are given and what we've learned? Who is the doer? Who is the hearer? What is the outcome of doing?

5. The **doer** of the work is blessed in his **deed** according to verse 25. The blessing comes from the doing not from what we receive from the doing. It is a matter of simple obedience. What promises do we find that come from being an obedient doer of the work?

   a. Psalm 19:9–11

   b. Psalm 119:1–3

   c. John 13:17

JAMES 1:22–27   56   LESSON #6

    d. Revelation 22:13, 14

6. Is there an area of your life that the Lord is specifically speaking to you about today? Is there something you need to allow Him to change? Will you surrender it to Him in prayer today? Record your prayer here or in a personal journal.

DAY 5—BEGIN IN PRAYER

1. Read James 1:22–27.

2. Re-read James 1:26, 27.

3. James has powerfully taught us that if we are merely **hearers** of the Word, we have deluded ourselves. We must also be **doers** of the Word. Now he takes us one step further in warning us of the self-deception of thinking that the mere act of doing **religious works** can substitute for true works of love. James lists three specific areas of our lives that we can use to evaluate the purity of our relationship. What are they?

    1.

    2.

    3.

4. In verse 26 we have the picture of a man who **seems** (thinks himself, in his own estimation) to be religious, but the evidence that his actions are only

outwardly pious is proven by his uncontrolled tongue. What more can we learn about how our words reveal our true self?

    a. Proverbs 10:20

    b. Proverbs 10:31

    c. Proverbs 15:28

    d. Matthew 12:34, 35

5. James stresses that the commitment to personal service and personal purity are outward signs of the truly devoted believer. The ministering to the desperately needy of society (the orphans and widows of James time) is a very real responsibility of the believer. How are you more motivated toward hands on service through the study of the following Scriptures?

    a. Psalms 41:1–3

    b. Proverbs 28:27

    c. Matthew 10:41, 42

    d. Matthew 25:34–40

JAMES 1:22-27 — **LESSON #6**

Lastly, as believers, we are to be in the world, but not of it. We are to keep ourselves "unspotted (**unstained; unpolluted; undefiled**) from the world." What does this mean in our practical, everyday living?

God sets us apart for Himself, preserves and keeps us holy. Read and meditate on 1Thessalonians 5:23, 24 and Jude 24, 25. It is our responsibility to cooperate with the Holy Spirit and allow Him to work in us.

6. Is there an area of your life that the Lord is specifically speaking to you about today? Is there something you need to allow Him to change? Will you surrender it to Him in prayer today? Record your prayer here or in a personal journal.

DAY 6—BEGIN IN PRAYER

1. Read James 1:22-27.

2. In what area of your life have you been strengthened most from your study this week?

3. Have you been more active at **doing** what the Lord has taught you this week? Share with the group, if you desire.

4. Have you taken notice of your tongue this week? What has it revealed about your relationship with the Lord?

5. Are you compelled by your love for the Lord to help the needy and flee the sinful staining of the world? Ask the Lord in prayer to draw you closer and more in love with Him.

> But be ye doers of the word, and not hearers only, deceiving your own selves. James 1:22

JAMES 2:1-13 — LESSON #7

DAY 1—BEGIN IN PRAYER

1. Read James 2:1-13.

2. What is James' main point in these verses?

3. What do you think "respect of persons" means? Is "respect of persons" a problem in our churches today? How?

   Optional: Use your Dictionary of New Testament Words or Strong's Concordance to find the meaning of the Greek word translated "respect of persons" in verse 1?

4. As believers, we need to examine our own hearts in light of this direction from God's Word. Ask the Lord in prayer to keep your heart teachable and your spirit open to His direction as you study these verses this week. Record your prayer here.

5. Choose a verse to memorize this week. Begin working on it today. **Do not neglect this important step in making the Word part of your life.**

DAY 2—BEGIN IN PRAYER

1. Read James 2:1-13.

2. Re-read James 2:1-4.

©2001—Morningstar Christian Chapel, Whittier, CA

3. James teaches us that true faith abolishes discrimination. It is very common in the world and a huge part of our **old nature** to judge or make a decision about others based on outward appearance. What do we learn about God's character, His nature in regards to His dealing with mankind?

   a. Deuteronomy 10:17, 18

   b. 2Chronicles 19:7

   c. Romans 2:11

   d. Ephesians 6:9

4. When we proclaim faith in the Lord Jesus Christ, the Lord of Glory, we cannot, and must not, allow our judgment of others to be superficial, prejudiced or based on any factor other than the blood of Jesus Christ sacrificed for our sins. It has been said, **"the ground is level at the cross."** How then must we **think** and **act** in relation to one another?

   a. Leviticus 19:15

   b. Proverbs 24:23

   c. Galatians 3:28

JAMES 2:1–13   LESSON #7

    d. Colossians 3:10–13

5. James gives us this illustration of the rich man and the poor man who were met by an usher who immediately passed judgment about their value based on their clothes. What conclusion is made about the truth in our hearts if we continually practice partiality towards others (v. 4)?

    Read 1Peter 1:17–22 with this sin of "respect of persons" in mind. How will it make you judge differently this week?

6. Is there an area of your life that the Lord is specifically speaking to you about today? Is there something you need to allow Him to change? Will you surrender it to Him in prayer today? Record your prayer here or in a personal journal.

Day 3—Begin in Prayer

1. Read James 2:1–13.

2. Re-read James 2:5–7.

3. Notice the compassion James uses when he needs to point out the failure and sin of his brethren. We need to realize that when it is necessary to bring correction, it needs to always be with a heart of love and compassion. James says literally, "has not God chosen those who are poor in the world's estimation." There is a tremendous difference in those things that the world values and what **truly** is of value. What measuring scale do we find in the Word regarding those things that are truly valuable?

    a. Isaiah 55:8, 9

b. Matthew 6:19–21; 33

c. 1 Timothy 6:7, 8

d. Hebrews 13:5, 6

4. This statement regarding God's choosing the **poor** in no way means that all poor people will be saved or if you are poor you have God's favor. Rather, generally speaking, those who have **less** materially often come face-to-face with their spiritual emptiness more readily. Why do you think that this is often the case? What would easily keep the rich person from seeking God?

What do these Scriptures teach us about the deceptive nature of the riches of this world?

a. Matthew 13:22

b. Matthew 19:24–26

c. 1 Timothy 6:9, 10

JAMES 2:1–13 — LESSON #7

5. We are often compelled by our flesh to cater to the rich and powerful of this world even while they continue to blaspheme the worthy name by which we are called. What are some ways that the world degrades and tramples on the name of Christ and the believers that follow Him—**Christians**?

   Compare 2Corinthians 6:14–18 with John 17:15, how can we be **separate** from the world but still be **in** the world?

6. Is there an area of your life that the Lord is specifically speaking to you about today? Is there something you need to allow Him to change? Will you surrender it to Him in prayer today? Record your prayer here or in a personal journal.

Day 4—Begin in Prayer

1. Read James 2:1–13. **(It is important!)**

2. Re-read James 2:8–11.

3. Anticipating the objection: "I was doing it to show God's love," we are given a standard by the Lord which to evaluate our actions. "If you fulfill the royal law...you do well." What do we learn about "the royal law"?

   a. Leviticus 19:18

   b. Mark 12:29–31

   c. Romans 13:8–10

JAMES 2:1-13 LESSON #7

4. Read Jesus' example of the **true neighbor** in Luke 10:25-37. Take into account the cultural prejudice and relate this story to our present day temptation to be a "respector of persons."

Personal: The Lord calls us all to self-examination. Are you reaching out to those who have nothing to benefit you? Or only those which may profit you? Do you show respect to some and reject others not considering God's choosing of them? It is sin, like unto murder!

5. The lesson we need to take to heart is that the Law is broken just as severely when we fail to love others (becoming a "respector of persons") as when we fail to obey the commands: "do not kill or do not commit adultery." How do the following Scriptures help you to fulfill "the royal law"?

   a. Galatians 5:13-16

   b. Galatians 6:8-10

   c. Romans 8:3-6

   d. 1Peter 1:22

6. Is there an area of your life that the Lord is specifically speaking to you about today? Is there something you need to allow Him to change? Will you surrender it to Him in prayer today? Record your prayer here or in a personal journal.

JAMES 2:1–13 — LESSON #7

DAY 5—BEGIN IN PRAYER

1. Read James 2:1–13.

2. Re-read James 2:12, 13.

3. As believers, instead of showing preferences, we need to carefully act toward others according to that immeasurable mercy we have been given. God's mercy, freely given, allows us to be free from the bondage of sin and its penalty: death. What description of this freedom and forgiveness do we find in these Scriptures?

    a. Luke 4:16–18

    b. John 5:24

    c. John 8:36

    d. Romans 8:1, 2

4. The judgment spoken of in verse 12 refers to the judgment of believers standing before the judgment seat of Christ. It **does not** refer to salvation, but to the motives, attitudes and actions of the believer. What do we learn about this judgment and how it would relate to the subject of our love and actions towards others?

    a. Romans 14:10–13

JAMES 2:1–13   LESSON #7

    b. 1Corinthians 3:12–15

    c. 2Corinthians 5:9, 10

5.   Define the term **mercy**?

    What do we learn about God's mercy upon our lives?

    a. Micah 7:18

    b. Psalm 86:5

    c. Psalm 103:17, 18

    d. Ephesians 2:4–6

    e. Titus 3:3–6

JAMES 2:1–13 — LESSON #7

6. Is there an area of your life that the Lord is specifically speaking to you about today? Is there something you need to allow Him to change? Will you surrender it to Him in prayer today? Record your prayer here or in a personal journal.

DAY 6—BEGIN IN PRAYER

1. Read James 2:1–13.

2. In what way do you view differently the practice of being a **respector of persons?**

3. What law **must** control our lives and actions toward others?

4. How does this passage affect our ability to show honor or appreciation to others?

    a. 1 Thessalonians 5:12, 13

    b. Philippians 2:29, 30

5. Read Matthew 18:21–35. **How are you doing at being merciful and forgiving debt?**

6. Have you completed your memory verse this week? **If not, do so today.**

> My brethren, have not the faith of our Lord Jesus Christ, the Lord of glory, with respect of persons. James 2:1

©2001—Morningstar Christian Chapel, Whittier, CA

68

JAMES 2:14–20 LESSON #8

DAY 1—BEGIN IN PRAYER

1. Read James 2:14–20.

2. In your own words give a summary of the teaching from James 2:14–20.

3. A key word in verse 14 is the word **say**. What does it profit a man if he **says** he has faith but his life does not show any evidence of that faith? Can you give a **general** example of this common tendency to say and not do?

4. Someone has said, **"Paul and James do not stand face-to-face fighting against each other, but back to back fighting opposite foes."** Plainly, Paul emphasizes the root of faith: what happens when we believe; while James emphasizes the fruit of faith: what happens after salvation. Paul's perspective is God's part, James' is the obvious, visible effects of salvation in our lives. How are we truly saved? Do our good works impart salvation to our lives?

   a. Ephesians 2:8, 9

   b. 2Timothy 1:9

   c. Titus 3:5

5. Choose a verse to memorize this week. Begin working on it now.

DAY 2—BEGIN IN PRAYER

1. Read James 2:14–20.

©2001—MORNINGSTAR CHRISTIAN CHAPEL, WHITTIER, CA

JAMES 2:14-20　　　　　　　　70　　　　　　　　LESSON #8

2. Re-read James 2:14.

3. James definitely does not speak of the man who has the real faith in Jesus Christ, but of the one who **says**, who **declares**, that he has such faith. There is all the difference in the world between the two. A **professor** of faith in Jesus Christ may not **possess** it. What revealing truth do we find in the following teaching in Matthew 7:15-23?

4. **Saying** is not truly believing. Jesus says in Matthew: "he who **does** the will of His Father will enter into the kingdom of heaven." What warnings do we find in the following Scriptures that cause us to examine our heart?

   a. 1 Samuel 15:22, 23

   b. Isaiah 1:11-17

   c. Isaiah 29:13

   d. Titus 1:16

5. James' rhetorical question in verse 14 asks us this, what profit is there in **saying** and is that **enough?** If we truly have experienced the new birth, salvation that comes from trusting Jesus Christ as our Lord and Savior, then there is no way that we can hide the effects of that salvation in our thoughts, words and actions. What is this fruit that will appear because of **true faith?**

   a. Psalms 1:1-3

JAMES 2:14–20 — LESSON #8

   b. Galatians 5:22–26

   c. Ephesians 5:9–11

   d. Philippians 1:9–11

6. Is there an area of your life that the Lord is specifically speaking to you about today? Is there something you need to allow Him to change? Will you surrender it to Him in prayer today? Record your prayer here or in a personal journal.

DAY 3—BEGIN IN PRAYER

1. Read James 2:14–20.

2. Re-read James 2:15, 16.

3. James gives us a graphic illustration of how this **professed faith** shows itself in our churches. If a brother or sister is without necessary clothing or destitute of daily food and our reaction is, "I'll pray for you," when we have means to meet their need, our faith is severely lacking. Read this parable in Luke 10:30–37, what insight do we gain about the one who is truly the neighbor?

   Compare this passage with 1John 3:16–19.

JAMES 2:14-20 — LESSON #8

Personal: How are you doing at revealing your faith to the world?

4. Verbal faith is cheap, whereas genuine faith produces works of compassion reflecting the heart of Jesus. Record what you learn from the following references regarding our responsibility to live out our faith in the body and in the world.

   a. Hebrews 10:24

   b. 1Timothy 6:18, 19

   c. Titus 2:7-10

   d. 1Peter 2:12

5. What may keep us from being sensitive and willing to meet the physical needs of those in the Body of Christ?

   a. Ezekiel 33:30-32

   b. Luke 12:15

   c. 1Timothy 6:7-10

JAMES 2:14–20   LESSON #8

d. Matthew 6:31–34

6. Is there an area of your life that the Lord is specifically speaking to you about today? Is there something you need to allow Him to change? Will you surrender it to Him in prayer today? Record your prayer here or in a personal journal.

DAY 4—BEGIN IN PRAYER (Don't forget Who the teacher is!)

1. Read James 2:14–20.

2. Re-read James 2:17, 18.

3. What conclusion is drawn about this **professed** faith without actions?

   Look up the definition of this word **dead**, what insight does this definition give us about the heart of the man who **says** he has faith?

4. A living faith has to bear fruit, it has to produce works of compassion toward others that are tangible, not merely sweet words. This fruit-bearing process is described in detail in John 15. Record the truth found in each verse regarding our responsibility in the fruit-bearing process.

   a. Verse 3

   b. Verse 4

c. Verse 5

d. Verse 7

e. Verse 8

5. James anticipates an objection to this truth, but someone will say, "thou hast faith, and I have works," James' response, "shew me thy faith without thy works, and I will shew thee my faith by my works." The question to be answered is, how can something invisible be seen? The word to **shew** means: **to declare; to exhibit; expose to the eyes; to give evidence or proof of a thing**. What direction are we given concerning the **works** that bear witness of our salvation?

a. Matthew 5:16

b. Colossians 1:9, 10

c. Titus 3:8

d. Titus 3:14

Challenge: Do you want to see faith in action? Read Hebrews 11 this week.

JAMES 2:14–20 — LESSON #8

6. Is there an area of your life that the Lord is specifically speaking to you about today? Is there something you need to allow Him to change? Will you surrender it to Him in prayer today? Record your prayer here or in a personal journal.

We sometimes forget that there are two kinds of witnesses—witnesses for Christ and witnesses against Him. Certainly the one who just professes Christ without living Him in his daily life is a witness against Him.
—Spiros Zodhiates – The Labor of Love

Day 5—Begin in Prayer

1. Read James 2:14–20.

2. Re-read James 2:19, 20.

3. James makes reference to Deuteronomy 6:4: "Hear O Israel: The Lord our God is one Lord." This verse does not say that this man believed **in** God, but that there is one God, or that God is one. His faith is an intellectual one, it is head knowledge, which never changes the disposition of the heart. There is a belief that is not true faith. What do we learn from the life of Simon, the sorcerer, regarding those who profess to believe yet show no fruit?

    a. Acts 8:13

    b. Acts 8:18–23

4. James tells us that there are no atheists among the demon population. Not only do they **also** believe (intellectual faith), they tremble. The word **tremble** means: **to bristle; stiffen; to stand up; to shudder; to be struck with extreme fear; to be horrified.** They believe that Jesus is God and it causes

them great terror, but it is **not** a saving experience. Record the declarations of the enemy when confronted with the Lord Jesus Christ.

a. Matthew 8:29-32

b. Mark 1:23, 24

Note: James says that the devils "also, in like manner," **believe**. Their belief is equated with the man who professes faith but has no fruit to back up his words.

5. James concludes this portion of Scripture with a plea, "But wilt thou know, O vain man, that faith without works is dead?" Or, will you conclude that professing to have faith when there is no fruit in your life to document that profession is empty and useless. It takes more than intellectual assent, more than an emotional response, to be truly saved. James makes an appeal to the **will** of man, do you really **want** to know?

What brings true saving faith (according to the Word of God)?

a. John 3:16-18

b. John 6:29

c. Romans 10:9, 10

d. 1John 5:1, 2

JAMES 2:14–20 — LESSON #8

Now use your Dictionary of New Testament Words or Strong's Bible Concordance to define "believe" in one of the above verses.

6. Is there an area of your life that the Lord is specifically speaking to you about today? Is there something you need to allow Him to change? Will you surrender it to Him in prayer today? Record your prayer here or in a personal journal.

Day 6—Begin in Prayer

1. Read James 2:14–20.

2. How have you been encouraged or challenged this week through this portion of James?

3. Take some time today to examine the fruit in your life. Look back over the last month, is there obvious fruit being produced from an intimate walk with the Lord?

   How do you love?

JAMES 2:14–20   78   LESSON #8

How fruitful in joy, peace, patience, goodness, meekness, self-control is your life?

Is it obvious to those around you that God lives in your life? If you see someone in need, are you willing to help?

4. How is true saving faith, a life totally surrendered and entrusted to the care of the Lord Jesus Christ, different from that of the man described in verse 14?

5. Have you completed your memory verse this week? **If not, do so today.** Why not share it with someone else!

Even so faith, if it hath not works, is dead, being alone. James 2:17

F = FORSAKING
A = ALL
I = I
T = TAKE
H = HIM

JAMES 2:21–26 — LESSON #9

DAY 1 — BEGIN IN PRAYER

1. Read James 2:21–26.

2. The great expanse between the **profession** of faith and the **action** of faith in the church is the subject of this continuation of James' lesson. Define what James means when he uses the words:

   a. Faith

   b. Works

3. James proceeds to give us two very opposite illustrations of the truth that a mere profession of faith is **dead** (**idle; empty; vain**). Who are they? What is different about their lives? What is the same?

4. Use an Expository Dictionary or a Strong's Concordance to define the following words:

   a. Justified (v. 21)

   b. Perfect (v. 22)

JAMES 2:21–26   LESSON #9

    c. Imputed (v. 23)

5. Choose a verse to memorize this week. Begin working on it today.

> I delight to do thy will, O my God: yea, thy law is within my heart.
> Psalms 40:8

Day 2—Begin in Prayer

1. Read James 2:21–26.

2. Re-read James 2:21.

3. Now James asks his listeners and readers a rhetorical question which, according to Greek scholars, he truly expects an affirmative answer. "Was not Abraham our father justified (declared righteous) by his works, when he offered Isaac his son upon the altar?" Briefly record the details of this account in Genesis 22:1–19.

    What did Abraham's **actions prove** about his relationship to God?

4. Now read and record the details of Abraham's encounter with the LORD over 40 years **earlier** in Genesis 15:1–6. What caused him to be accounted righteous?

Read Hebrews 11:17. How did Abraham offer up Isaac?

When did Abraham receive the promise that God would make him "a nation more than the stars of the heavens or the sands of the sea"—prior to the birth of Isaac or when he was called to offer Isaac?

Was Abraham **saved** before offering Isaac? Do you think James knew that? How?

5. James' use of Abraham as an illustration that true saving faith will be **demonstrated to be genuine** by **actions** is supported in John 8:39. In this passage Jesus confronts some who **said** they were Abraham's children. What was Jesus' response to them?

Personal: What has the fruit or works in your life declared about your relationship with the Lord today?

6. Is there an area of your life that the Lord is specifically speaking to you about today? Is there something you need to allow Him to change? Will you surrender it to Him in prayer today? Record your prayer here or in a personal journal.

DAY 3—BEGIN IN PRAYER

1. Read James 2:21–26.

2. Re-read James 2:22–24.

JAMES 2:21–26 — LESSON #9

3. James continues with his urgent plea, "Do you see," your faith must result in action to be real and when they are displayed together they bring faith to full maturity. In order for our faith to reach this point of maturity we must learn to walk in obedience to the Word of God—rejecting the urging of the flesh and the counsel of the world. What insight do we find in the following Scriptures that teaches us that for the true believer in Jesus Christ, obedience is the natural outcome and proof of relationship?

   a. 1Samuel 15:22

   b. Psalm 51:16, 17

   c. Romans 6:16–18

   d. 1John 2:3–6

4. In order for Abraham to walk in obedience to God's will he was required to daily surrender his will to the control of his Heavenly Father. He was convinced of God's awesome love and His ability to care for his life perfectly. This brought him this testimony, **"he was called the Friend of God."** What do we learn about this necessary process of surrender in our lives?

   a. Romans 6:12, 13

   b. Romans 13:13, 14

JAMES 2:21–26   LESSON #9

    c. Galatians 5:24

    d. 1John 2:15–17

    Personal: Are you called a friend of Jesus? See John 15:14.

5. Walking in the Spirit means daily (moment by moment) making a choice to choose God's way not our way. Use the following Scriptures as a test of your walk in the Spirit.

    a. Matthew 16:24, 25

    b. Mark 11:25, 26

    c. John 13:34, 35

    d. Romans 15:1, 2

By faith, Abraham was justified **before God** and his righteousness declared; by works, he was justified **before men** and his righteousness demonstrated.
—Warren Wiersbe – The Bible Exposition Commentary

JAMES 2:21-26 — LESSON #9

6. Is there an area of your life that the Lord is specifically speaking to you about today? Is there something you need to allow Him to change? Will you surrender it to Him in prayer today? Record your prayer here or in a personal journal.

Day 4—Begin in Prayer

1. Read James 2:21-26.

2. Re-read James 2:25.

3. So that we might understand that everyone, from every social class, every walk of life, needs to come to the same saving faith, James gives us the extreme opposite example—the life and faith of Rahab. Read Joshua 2:1-21 and record the details of Rahab's life.

    a. What had she heard?

    b. What was the effect in her life?

    c. What declaration of faith did she make about God?

    d. What does the summary of Rahab's life in Hebrews 11:31 say about her faith and what it caused her to **do?**

4. What do the following verses reveal about Rahab's life after being saved?

    a. Joshua 6:25

b. Matthew 1:1; 5, 6 (Rahab-Rachab) (Booz-Boaz)

c. Ruth 4:21, 22

5. Even though Rahab's earthly biography describes her as a harlot, how does God see her? How does He see you in Christ?

   a. Isaiah 1:18

   b. 2Corinthians 5:17

   c. Ephesians 1:3-7

   d. Ephesians 2:4-7

   Since this is true, our lives ought to brilliantly display the good works that bring glory to God! Matthew 5:16

JAMES 2:21–26   LESSON #9

6. Is there an area of your life that the Lord is specifically speaking to you about today? Is there something you need to allow Him to change? Will you surrender it to Him in prayer today? Record your prayer here or in a personal journal.

DAY 5—BEGIN IN PRAYER

1. Read James 2:21–26.

2. Re-read James 2:26.

3. James rests his point with one lasting analogy. "For a body without a spirit is dead, so faith without works is dead also." If you picture "faith without works" as comparable to a corpse, you get the full emphasis of the teaching of James. He understood, and so ought we now, that real faith is potent, it always and continually produces good works. Turn to Hebrews 11 and complete the following chart:

How	Who	What Action
v. 4 – By Faith	Abel	Offered
v. 7 – By Faith		
v. 8 – By Faith		
v. 20 – By Faith		
v. 21 – By Faith		
v. 22 – By Faith		
v. 23 – By Faith		
v. 24 – By Faith		
v. 31 – By Faith		

4. What do we learn from the following references about those who profess to know God?

JAMES 2:21–26   87   LESSON #9

    a. Titus 1:16

    b. Matthew 7:21–23

5. With what attitude are we to serve the Lord and do the work He has called us to do?
    a. Psalm 100:2–4

    b. Colossians 3:17

    c. Ephesians 6:5–8

6. Is there an area of your life that the Lord is specifically speaking to you about today? Is there something you need to allow Him to change? Will you surrender it to Him in prayer today? Record your prayer here or in a personal journal.

DAY 6—BEGIN IN PRAYER

1. Read James 2:21–26.

2. The point James wants us to understand is that we **cannot** hold the faith of Jesus Christ in hypocrisy. A hypocrite, like a dead body, is offensive. Offensive to God and to others. To pretend to be something we are not, God cannot stand and neither can those who live with us. In one word sum up what Jesus said to those who tried to fool God with their pretense of holiness in Matthew 23?

JAMES 2:21–26 — LESSON #9

3. Read and meditate on 1Corinthians 3:12–15. How does it speak to your life?

4. How has your faith been proven to be genuine by your actions today? Think about it as you continue through your day.

5. Lastly, how are you doing on that memory verse? **Complete it today.**

For as the body without the spirit is dead, so faith without works is dead also. James 2:26

JAMES 1–2 REVIEW — LESSON #10

DAY 1—BEGIN IN PRAYER (Remember Who the teacher is!)

1. Read James 1–2. **(Slowly and prayerfully!)**

2. Record the main subjects in the following divisions of James:

   a. James 1:1–12

   b. James 1:13–27

   c. James 2:1–13

   d. James 2:14–26

3. Record the Scriptures that minister to you new and afresh today.

4. Use Philippians 2:13 as a springboard for prayer asking the Lord to make you a "doer of the Word" by the work of the Holy Spirit within your life.

DAY 2—BEGIN IN PRAYER

1. Read James 1:1–12.

©2001—Morningstar Christian Chapel, Whittier, CA

JAMES 1–2 REVIEW — LESSON #10

2. Remember the first chapter of James deals with two types of **temptations:** those that come from without; and those that come from within. This first portion of the chapter deals with temptations that come from outside sources.

   a. Does this word "temptation" mean a seduction to sin?

   b. How are we to "count"; **consider**; and **view** these trials?

   c. What is the purpose of "trials" in the life of the believer?

3. The attitude with which we face these trials determines the outcome and the effect they have on our lives. Record the attitudes of those who face trials described in the following Scriptures:

   a. Habakkuk 3:17–19

   b. 2Corinthians 12:9, 10

   c. Hebrews 12:2, 3

   d. 1Peter 4:12, 13

JAMES 1–2 REVIEW — LESSON #10

Optional: Share a time when a trial faced with joy brought spiritual growth in your life and brought glory and honor to your Heavenly Father.

4. When trials of various kinds come into our lives, and they will, we are in need of wisdom from the Lord in order to respond correctly. What did you learn about God's wisdom from James 1:5–8?

   There is a promise in verse 5 to those who need wisdom in the face of trials. What is it?

   Why do you think it is important that we "ask in faith, nothing wavering"?

5. When we face trials in our lives it is absolutely necessary that we have our eyes fixed on the eternal perspective. We need to view our lives with the Lord's perfect purpose in mind. How does James encourage us to keep eternity in view?

   Personal: How are you doing with the trials you are facing today? Are you looking at the trial or the Lord Who has your perfection and maturity as His first priority?

Day 3—Begin in Prayer

1. Read James 1:13–27.

JAMES 1–2 REVIEW — LESSON #10

2. The second type of **temptation** that James teaches us about is that which comes from within. When we are faced with this temptation, we need to understand it's origin. "God cannot be tempted with evil, neither tempteth He any man:" This temptation is a solicitation to evil and we cannot and must not blame it on God. Record the progression of temptation according to verses 14, 15.

3. What do we learn from the following Scriptures that will help us resist the temptation of the flesh and the enemy?

   a. 2Corinthians 10:3-5

   b. Philippians 4:8, 9

   c. 2Peter 1:3-8

4. James 1:22 is considered to be the key verse of the book of James. The key verse is that which best sums up the message. In your own words, what does being a **doer** of the Word mean? How does the **hearer** deceive himself? Does the **hearer usually** deceive anyone else?

5. We are not able to be a "doer of the Word" in our own strength. According to the following Scriptures what enables us to walk uprightly before the Lord?

   a. Psalm 37:30, 31

JAMES 1–2 REVIEW — LESSON #10

b. Psalm 119:9–11

c. Luke 11:1–4

d. Acts 1:8

e. Ephesians 4:11–14

We all,...beholding...the glory of the Lord, are being transformed into the same image from glory to glory. 2Corinthians 3:18

Personal: Are you diligently beholding the glory of the Lord?

DAY 4—BEGIN IN PRAYER

1. Read James 2:1–13.

JAMES 1–2 REVIEW — LESSON #10

2. This portion of chapter 2 deals with one basic subject. What is it?

3. Who is **most** affected by this sinful behavior of being a respector of persons?

4. What message does God want us to give all men regardless of their social status or their nationality?

   a. John 3:16–18

   b. Acts 2:21

   c. Romans 10:12, 13

   d. Galatians 3:28

5. What is the "royal law"? And how would fulfilling it prevent us from committing the sin of having respect of persons?

Personal: Do you truly see that being a respector of persons is sin? How will this effect your dealing with others today?

JAMES 1–2 REVIEW — LESSON #10

DAY 5—BEGIN IN PRAYER

1. Read James 2:14–26.

2. Using James' description, describe the faith of the man who is professing to trust in Jesus Christ as his Savior and Lord and yet there is no fruit in his life to prove out his profession. (Give reference for each.)

3. James asks us, what profit is there in the life of one who says he has faith and has not works (fruit)? Can this profession save him? What do you think? Is it good enough to say, "I believe there is a God"?

   Challenge: Find two verses that quote Jesus using fruit (works) as proof of true faith?

   a.

   b.

4. What did Abraham and Rahab do that demonstrated to us that they truly **believed (to be persuaded of; to rely on; to place confidence in)** God?

5. Share an example of someone you know that strongly declares the validity of their salvation by their lifestyle and actions.

   Personal: What fruit has developed in your life that is proof to you that you have saving faith?

JAMES 1–2 REVIEW — LESSON #10

DAY 6—BEGIN IN PRAYER

1. Read James 1–2.

2. The study of James causes us to be unable to continue **saying without doing** in our Christian walks. How has your walk been changed by the study of James 1–2?

3. Paul calls us to examine ourselves, "whether we be in the faith," (2Corinthians 13:5). Consider the answers to the following questions in examination of your own faith:

    a. Was there a time when I honestly realized I was a sinner and admitted this to myself and to God?

    b. Was there a time when my heart stirred me to flee from the wrath to come?

    c. Do I truly understand the Gospel, that Christ died for my sins and arose again? Do I understand and confess that I cannot save myself?

    d. Did I sincerely repent of my sins and turn from them? Or do I secretly love sin?

    e. Have I trusted Christ and Christ alone for my salvation? Do I enjoy a living relationship with Him through the Word and in the Spirit?

JAMES 1–2 REVIEW — LESSON #10

f. Has there been a change in my life? Can others tell that I have been with Jesus?

g. Do I desire to share Christ with others? Or am I ashamed of Him?

h. Do I enjoy the fellowship of God's people?

i. Is worship a delight to me?

j. Am I ready for the Lord's return?

As we complete this portion of James, will you agree in prayer with the Psalmist:

> Search me, O God, and know my heart: try me, and know my thoughts: And see if there be any wicked way in me, and lead me in the way everlasting. Psalms 139:23, 24

Faith alone saves, but the faith that saves is not alone. — J. Calvin

REVIEW & OVERVIEW
JAMES 3:1-4

LESSON #11

DAY 1—BEGIN IN PRAYER

1. Read James 1–2. **(Slowly and prayerfully!)**

2. Record the main subjects in the following divisions of James:

   a. James 1:1–12

   b. James 1:13–27

   c. James 2:1–13

   d. James 2:14–26

3. James has detailed two characteristics of the mature believer in these two chapters. In a few words, how would you summarize them?

   a. Chapter 1

   b. Chapter 2

REVIEW & OVERVIEW
JAMES 3:1-4
LESSON #11

4. Read James chapters 3-5 and give a Title to each of the chapters. (Title = 5-6 word description of the contents that will help you to remember the subject matter.)

   a. Chapter 3

   b. Chapter 4

   c. Chapter 5

5. Choose a verse from James 3:1-4 to use as a memory verse this week. Begin working on it today.

DAY 2—BEGIN IN PRAYER

1. Read James 3:1-4.

2. Re-read James 3:1.

3. James begins chapter 3 with an exhortation and a warning. It seems that many in the early church thought that the best thing to do was to **teach (or voice their opinion).** James warns that this willingness to **share** was of great cause for concern because of the potential for sin that is inherent in the use of the tongue. What is the correct motive and reason for a believer to be willing to teach?

   a. 1Corinthians 12:27-31

REVIEW & OVERVIEW
JAMES 3:1-4

LESSON #11

  b. Ephesians 4:11-13

  c. 1Corinthians 9:16

  d. 1Thessalonians 2:4

  e. John 21:15-17

  f. 1Peter 5:2-4

4. James tells us that with this calling to teach comes a greater judgment. Why is this so (use Romans 2:21-24 to help with your answer) and how is this a warning to us who proclaim ourselves Christians?

5. You may not be in a church pulpit or a teacher of hundreds but are you a teacher of God's Word. Have you ever opened the Word to share with your family, a neighbor or your children? How is your life to reflect Christ so that others will desire to follow Him?

  a. Matthew 5:14-16

  b. Philippians 2:14-16

©2001—Morningstar Christian Chapel, Whittier, CA

c. 1Peter 2:9-15

6. What area of your life has the Lord spoken to you about today? Is there something you need to allow Him to change? Allow Him to mold you into His image today by willingly giving Him your heart and life to use for His glory. Record your prayer here or in a personal journal.

Day 3—Begin in Prayer

1. Read James 3:1-4.

2. Re-read James 3:2.

3. We are reminded of the frequency and diversity of our sin. In many things we sin and we do so in many ways. James includes himself and everyone else, "all have sinned." What direction do we receive regarding the use of this potentially lethal weapon between our teeth?

    a. Psalm 34:13

    b. Psalm 39:1

    c. Proverbs 12:19; 22

    d. Proverbs 18:21

REVIEW & OVERVIEW
JAMES 3:1–4

LESSON #11

4. If we were able to **bridle (to guide; to hold in check; to restrain)** our tongue, it would be a mark of our maturity in the Lord. To "be perfect" means to **be mature, to have met the goal that has been set for us.** We are to strive toward maturity in our walk and the proof of our progress lies in the words we speak. What do we learn of this mark of Christian maturity?

   a. Proverbs 10:19–21

   b. Proverbs 15:28

   c. Proverbs 21:23

   d. Proverbs 23:15, 16

5. We cannot in our own strength and ability bridle our tongues. We must allow the Lord to take control and harness the power of the tongue. What then is the first step to taking control of our speech?

   a. Ezekiel 11:19, 20

   b. Ezekiel 36:26, 27

   c. John 3:3

REVIEW & OVERVIEW
JAMES 3:1–4

d. 2Corinthians 5:17–18

Personal: Have you been given a new heart, have you trusted Jesus Christ as your Lord and Savior? This is the first step in His transforming your life from the heart outward.

6. What area of your life has the Lord spoken to you about today? Is there something you need to allow Him to change? Allow Him to mold you into His image today by willingly giving Him your heart and life to use for His glory. Record your prayer here or in a personal journal.

DAY 4—BEGIN IN PRAYER

1. Read James 3:1–4.

2. Re-read James 3:3, 4.

3. James gives us two examples and exhorts us to **behold** the truths that we find in the comparisons. What are the two examples?

   What is the purpose of the bit and rudder?

   In order for the bit and the rudder to accomplish their purpose, what is required?

REVIEW & OVERVIEW
JAMES 3:1–4

LESSON #11

Record David's prayer in Psalm 141:3, 4a and make it the prayer of your heart today.

4. The bit in the horses' mouth and the rudder of a huge ship must both overcome contrary forces and both must be under the control of a strong hand. The human tongue must also overcome contrary forces; the old sin nature, circumstances around us and the temptation of the enemy. How much more we need to willingly surrender control of our lives to the strong firm guidance of the Lord's hand. Use the following Scriptures as a reminder what our words ought to accomplish.

   a. Psalm 71:23, 24

   b. Psalm 119:46

   c. Ephesians 4:29–32

   d. Colossians 4:5, 6

5. Compare the difference between these two accounts in Peter's life and record the miracle of being controlled and guided by the Holy Spirit of God.

   a. John 18:15–18; 25–27

   b. Acts 2:14–41

REVIEW & OVERVIEW
JAMES 3:1–4

LESSON #11

Personal: If you would like to, share a time when the Holy Spirit gave you the boldness to proclaim Jesus Christ as Lord and Savior. Ask Him to empower you today.

6. What area of your life has the Lord spoken to you about today? Is there something you need to allow Him to change? Allow Him to mold you into His image today by willingly giving Him your heart and life to use for His glory. Record your prayer here or in a personal journal.

DAY 5—BEGIN IN PRAYER

1. Read James 3:1–4.

2. Read Psalm 19:14. **Is this the prayer of your heart today?**

3. We need to realize that the Lord does know our every word, and our every thought. What do you learn about this truth that will cause you to think twice (or more) today **before** you speak?

   a. Ecclesiastes 12:14

   b. Matthew 12:36, 37

   c. Romans 14:10–12

   d. 1 Corinthians 4:5

©2001—MORNINGSTAR CHRISTIAN CHAPEL, WHITTIER, CA

REVIEW & OVERVIEW
JAMES 3:1-4
LESSON #11

4. Read Psalm 39 and outline God's method of controlling our tongue as illustrated through David's prayer.

   a. Verses 1-3

   b. Verses 4-6

   c. Verses 7-8

   d. Verses 9-13

5. Our words can have the power to direct and guide; for good or for evil. How can we use them to make a positive difference in our homes and to direct others to the Lord Jesus Christ? See Deuteronomy 11:18-21.

   Personal: How are you living out this direction in your life and home? Where is there room for improvement?

6. What area of your life has the Lord spoken to you about today? Is there something you need to allow Him to change? Allow Him to mold you into His image today by willingly giving Him your heart and life to use for His glory. Record your prayer here or in a personal journal.

REVIEW & OVERVIEW
JAMES 3:1–4

LESSON #11

DAY 6—BEGIN IN PRAYER

1. Read James 3–5. **Slowly, listening to the Holy Spirits' direction.**

2. Spend time in prayer about what you have learned this week. How is the Lord changing your life?

3. Have you completed your memory verse this week? There may be a pop-quiz!

Thy word have I hid in mine heart, that I might not sin against thee. Psalms 119:11

For in many things we offend all. If any man offend not in word, the same is a perfect man, and able also to bridle the whole body. James 3:2

JAMES 3:5-12 — LESSON #12

DAY 1—BEGIN IN PRAYER

1. Read James 3:5-12.

2. What part of James' teaching on the potential evil that can be produced by the tongue most effects your life today?

3. What is the motivating force behind the evil workings of the tongue of the human being?

4. What is James' declaration of this unnatural process of good and evil coming from the same source (v. 10)?

5. Record Luke 6:45 and keep it in mind this week as we study James' penetrating and convicting exposition on the tongue. **What are your words saying about the treasure in your heart?**

6. Choose a verse to memorize this week. Begin working on it today.

DAY 2—BEGIN IN PRAYER

1. Read James 3:5-12.

2. Re-read James 3:5, 6.

3. This tongue is a little member, it has great potential for good or for evil. James compares its evil potential to the destructive work of an out of control fire. **Have you ever seen its evil at work in your family, church, workplace or school?** What warnings do we discover about this destructive work of the tongue?

   a. Proverbs 16:27, 28

   b. Proverbs 22:10

   c. Proverbs 26:20-22

   Compare the above Scriptures with the results of this little member when controlled and guided by the Lord.

   a. Proverbs 15:23

   b. Proverbs 25:11, 12

4. James goes further and calls this frightful tool a "world of iniquity (evil)." It is smallest of many parts but able to "defile the whole body." Its sin affects every part of us and it has a destructive effect upon the lives of those with which we come into contact. What directions are we given with regard to the use of the tongue and its connection to our relationship with others?

   a. 1Peter 2:1

b. Ephesians 4:25

c. Colossians 3:8-10

5. It is not surprising that the fuel for this fire created by the tongue is from hell itself. What is the goal of Satan in your life? See John 10:10. Record the result of one lie in the lives of the following men and women of the Bible.

   a. Genesis 3:4-8

   b. Genesis 39:7-20

   c. 1Kings 21:7-13

Personal: Have you recently used your tongue to cause such a destructive fire in the life of another? The Lord requires repentance when His children sin and He is waiting to forgive when we come humbly before Him. (1John 1:9)

6. What area of your life has the Lord spoken to you about today? Is there something you need to allow Him to change? Allow Him to mold you into His image today by willingly giving Him your heart and life to use for His glory. Record your prayer here or in a personal journal.

JAMES 3:5–12 — LESSON #12

DAY 3—BEGIN IN PRAYER

1. Read James 3:5–12.

2. Re-read James 3:7, 8.

3. The truth about our tongue is that even though man can tame wild animals and bring into submission those whose nature is wild and unruly, we have no power to tame our own tongues. How then can this unruly member be brought under control?

    a. Psalm 5:1–3

    b. Psalm 19:14

    c. Psalm 139:23, 24

    d. Galatians 5:16

4. The tongue is a restless evil full of deadly cyanide. Like the deadliest poisons, subtle criticism and slander are like verbal venom which has done its work before the victim can react. How does this poison work within the Body to destroy individuals, families and ministries? As Christians, what are we to do when we realize that we have sinned against another?

5. Read and record Philippians 4:8. How would application of this Scripture have a significant impact on the words we speak?

JAMES 3:5–12 — LESSON #12

6. What area of your life has the Lord spoken to you about today? Is there something you need to allow Him to change? Allow Him to mold you into His image today by willingly giving Him your heart and life to use for His glory. Record your prayer here or in a personal journal.

DAY 4—BEGIN IN PRAYER

1. Read James 3:5–12.

2. Re-read James 3:9, 10.

3. James now brings us the practical application of this teaching: we, as God's children, cannot entertain this hypocrisy in our Christian lives. These inconsistencies are unacceptable and cannot be tolerated. In a few words, how does God view this sin of hypocrisy? See Matthew 23:1–33.

4. It is sin when we religiously worship God in our churches and walk out and speak evil of our brethren. Why does the Lord tell us that this **must not** happen? What do the following Scriptures teach us about the design and creation of man?

    a. Genesis 1:26, 27

    b. Genesis 5:1, 2

    c. Genesis 9:6

    d. Acts 17:26–28

JAMES 3:5-12 — LESSON #12

5. We are reminded by James that man is made in the image and likeness of God. What does the Bible teach us about the body of the believer that **must** affect what we think and say about each other?

   a. 1Corinthians 3:16, 17

   b. 1Corinthians 6:19

   c. Ephesians 2:20-22

   d. 1Peter 2:5

   Personal: Meditate on the truth of this Scripture as you go about your week— 1John 4:20, 21. Selah!

6. What area of your life has the Lord spoken to you about today? Is there something you need to allow Him to change? Allow Him to mold you into His image today by willingly giving Him your heart and life to use for His glory. Record your prayer here or in a personal journal.

DAY 5—BEGIN IN PRAYER

1. Read James 3:5-12.

2. Re-read James 3:11, 12.

JAMES 3:5–12　　　115　　　LESSON #12

3. Let's return to the portion of Scripture that we started with this week. Record the main points of Luke 6:43–49.

   a. What does the mouth prove about the contents of the heart?

   b. What is the outward proof that Jesus Christ truly is our Lord?

   c. What is the foundation on which you are building your life?

4. James' words cause us to evaluate our own lives. "Blessing and cursing" **must not** come from the same source. It is not possible in nature and we are required, as believers, to examine our lives and allow the Lord the access to cleanse our heart so that only good fruit will spring forth. Use the following references as a means of prayer allowing the Lord to purify your heart and, therefore, your speech.

   a. Psalms 26:1–3

   b. Psalms 51:9, 10

   c. Psalms 139:23, 24

JAMES 3:5-12 — LESSON #12

5. The Word of God is clear that when there is need of repentance and forgiveness we can freely come before the Lord to ask that He might mold and change our lives. Record Isaiah's encounter with the true, living, and holy God.

   a. Isaiah 6:5

   b. Isaiah 6:6, 7

   c. Isaiah 6:8

   Personal: Is it your heart's desire to have God purge the sin of your lips? Ask Him! Now, pray daily and specifically about how you speak...keep this in mind constantly. Discipline yourself to be slow to speak remembering these warnings of James, the tongue can be a tool of heaven or a tool of hell. Give God your tongue and become a vessel of honor.

6. What area of your life has the Lord spoken to you about today? Is there something you need to allow Him to change? Allow Him to mold you into His image today by willingly giving Him your heart and life to use for His glory. Record your prayer here or in a personal journal.

DAY 6—BEGIN IN PRAYER

1. Read James 3:5-12.

JAMES 3:5-12 — LESSON #12

2. One of the most pleasing ways we can make **good** use of this tool between our teeth is in praise and worship of our Lord and God. Read Psalm 145, slowly, praising the Lord with King David. Is there a specific verse that speaks the praise of your heart today?

3. Keep His awesome works of mercy and grace toward you at the forefront of your thoughts today. Use your tongue to praise Him verbally and often. Record your worship and praise here.

4. Have you completed your memory verse this week? **If not, do so today!**

> Out of the same mouth proceedeth blessing and cursing. My brethren, these things ought not so to be. James 3:10

118

JAMES 3:13–18   LESSON #13

DAY 1—BEGIN IN PRAYER

1. Read James 3:13–18.

2. In a few words, give the main details of this teaching on "wisdom."

3. What is the proof that "wisdom from above" is **not** being exercised?

4. Describe the "wisdom that is from above." Do you think it should be easy to determine which wisdom is in operation by examining the **results** of our choices and actions? What do you think hinders us from seeking God's wisdom instead of **worldly wisdom?**

5. Choose a verse to memorize this week. Begin working on it today. (Carry it with you and pull it out at red lights, in line, or when the need to exercise wisdom arises.)

DAY 2—BEGIN IN PRAYER

1. Read James 3:13–18.

3. James moves from the topic of the tongue and its potential for good or destructive evil to another attribute that demonstrates the maturity level of the believer. James begins, "Who is a wise man and endued with knowledge among you?" How will you and I be able to recognize this truly wise man?

4. The Scriptures identify four specific means by which the wisdom of God comes to us. What are they?

©2001—MORNINGSTAR CHRISTIAN CHAPEL, WHITTIER, CA

JAMES 3:13–18 — 120 — LESSON #13

#1 — a. Psalm 111:10

— b. Proverbs 9:10

#2 — c. 1Corinthians 2:1–10

— d. Colossians 2:2, 3

#3 — e. Psalms 119:97–100

— f. Colossians 3:16

#4 — g. 1Kings 3:7–12

— h. James 1:5

5. As believers, our "wisdom" is to be exhibited through "meekness." **Meekness is not weakness, cowardice, or timidity.** It is often defined as **awesome power under control**. Meekness is synonymous with humility because the root of wisdom is a profound understanding of the awesome power and holiness of God and the acknowledgment of our sinfulness. When we

recognize this truth and surrender our lives to God's control, the outcome is meekness of heart that is able to act in Godly wisdom. Record the description of our Lord and Savior as He walked among men?

a. Matthew 11:29

b. Matthew 12:18–20

c. Matthew 21:4, 5

d. Philippians 2:5–8

6. What area of your life has the Lord spoken to you about today? Is there something you need to allow Him to change? Allow Him to mold you into His image today by willingly giving Him your heart and life to use for His glory. Record your prayer here or in a personal journal.

Day 3—Begin in Prayer

1. Read James 3:13–18.

2. Re-read James 3:14.

3. Now James gives us the ugly description of what happens when "wisdom that is not from above" is being exercised. Define these two characteristics of worldly wisdom:

a. Bitter envying

JAMES 3:13-18 — LESSON #13

b. Strife

4. What does the Word of God tell us about these traits and our responsibility, as believers, not to entertain or harbor them in our hearts?

   a. Romans 1:29-32

   b. Romans 13:12-14

   c. 1Corinthians 3:1-3

   d. Galatians 5:19-26

5. James exhorts us to be honest with ourselves. If these qualities of worldly wisdom exist in our heart and life we must call sin—sin. We are not to act, pretend or deceive ourselves into thinking they are spiritual qualities. We are "not to lie against the truth." "Bitter envying and strife" are works of the flesh. How do the following references encourage you to examine your relationships and allow the Lord to make any needed changes?

   a. Philippians 2:3, 4

   b. 1Peter 2:1, 2

JAMES 3:13-18 — LESSON #13

6. What area of your life has the Lord spoken to you about today? Is there something you need to allow Him to change? Allow Him to mold you into His image today by willingly giving Him your heart and life to use for His glory. Record your prayer here or in a personal journal.

DAY 4—BEGIN IN PRAYER

1. Read James 3:13-18.

2. Re-read James 13:15, 16.

3. James now exposes the diabolical bloodline of the wisdom that is "not from above." List the three characteristics of pseudo-wisdom. Use the following Scriptures to give a better description of each of these types of false wisdom.

    a. **Earthly** – worldly – 1Corinthians 1:18-20

    b. **Sensual** – natural, unspiritual – 1Corinthians 2:14; Jude 1:18, 19

    c. **Devilish** – demonic – Genesis 3:1-5; John 8:44

4. The results of this worldly wisdom at work are clear and obvious to all who watch. False wisdom that is "not from above" produces envy and strife which results in "confusion and every evil work." Record the outcome of worldly wisdom from the following references. How does this compare to the state of the world today? How does it compare to your church and your life?

    a. Romans 1:21, 22

    b. 1Corinthians 3:3, 4

c. 1Corinthians 3:18-20

d. Philippians 3:18, 19

5. If envy, strife, confusion and every evil work are the outcome of practicing **worldly wisdom,** what are we obligated to do when we see its effect in our lives?

   a. Revelation 2:5

   b. 1John 1:9

   c. Matthew 5:23, 24

   d. Ephesians 4:21-32 **(Don't try to write this out. Record any area that needs change in your life.)**

6. What area of your life has the Lord spoken to you about today? Is there something you need to allow Him to change? Allow Him to mold you into His image today by willingly giving Him your heart and life to use for His glory. Record your prayer here or in a personal journal.

| JAMES 3:13–18 | LESSON #13 |

Day 5—Begin in Prayer

1. Read James 3:13–18.

2. Re-read James 3:17, 18.

3. Now we are given the description of true wisdom, "the wisdom that is from above." Use a Dictionary of New Testament Words or the Strong's Concordance to define the following words that describe "wisdom that is from above."

    a. Pure

    b. Peaceable

    c. Gentle

    d. Easy to be intreated (Reasonable)

    e. Full of mercy and good fruits

    f. Without partiality (Unwavering)

    g. Without hypocrisy

JAMES 3:13-18　　　　LESSON #13

4. The "wisdom that is from above is first pure." It is "pure" in the sense of being **undefiled**; it is **morally pure**. This purity comes when a person has been cleansed by Christ's blood, who Himself is pure. It is significant that **purity** is listed as the first characteristic of "wisdom that is from above." **First** indicates that purity is the key to all the others, and not just the first on the list. What do the following Scriptures teach and remind us regarding the call and obligation of the believer to live a life of purity?

   a. Philippians 1:9-11

   b. Ephesians 5:26, 27

   c. 1 Thessalonians 3:12, 13

   d. 1 Peter 1:14-16

5. As James concludes this passage on the comparison of true and false wisdom he outlines the end results of godly wisdom. The point being that the peacemaker who sows in peace will reap a harvest of righteousness. Righteousness cannot be produced in a climate of bitterness, self-ambition or a party-spirit driven by wisdom from below. As Christians, we must desire and seek after "wisdom that is from above." Read and consider the truth of Proverbs 3:13-18. What is the promise to the one who finds **true wisdom?**

6. What area of your life has the Lord spoken to you about today? Is there something you need to allow Him to change? Allow Him to mold you into His image today by willingly giving Him your heart and life to use for His glory. Record your prayer here or in a personal journal.

JAMES 3:13–18   **LESSON #13**

DAY 6—BEGIN IN PRAYER (Don't forget Who the teacher is!)

1. Read James 3:13–18.

2. From these verses in James give a description of the truly wise person.

3. What are the characteristics of **wisdom from below?**

Personal: Is there any bitter envying and strife in your heart? There is no use hiding the truth, the results will soon be obvious to everyone. Ask the Lord for forgiveness and allow Him to change you from the inside out.

4. Read and record Proverbs 24:3. What is the foundation of your house?

5. Have you completed your memory verse this week? **If not, do so today.**

> But the wisdom that is from above is first pure, then peaceable, gentle, and easy to be intreated, full of mercy and good fruits, without partiality, and without hypocrisy. James 3:17

JAMES 4:1–6   LESSON #14

DAY 1 — BEGIN IN PRAYER

1. Read James 4:1–6.

2. In a few words, what important issue does James focus upon that is still the root of problems in our lives and our churches today?

3. He gives us the answer to have victory over this sin, what is it?

4. Use a Dictionary of New Testament Words or Bible Concordance to define the following words:

   a. Lust (v. 1)

   b. Lust (v. 2)

   c. Amiss (v. 3)

   d. Consume (v. 3)

   e. Enmity (v. 4)

5. Choose a verse to memorize this week. Begin working on it today.

> Thy word is a lamp unto my feet, and a light unto my path.
> Psalms 119:105

DAY 2—BEGIN IN PRAYER

1. Read James 4:1–6.

2. Re-read James 4:1.

3. As we begin the fourth chapter of the book of James, he continues to call us to live the life of the true believer.

    We are to be the **doer** not just the **hearer** when it comes to the control of our desires and passions that when left to their natural end cause fights and quarrels among us and in our churches. Record the Biblical description of this fighting and quarreling and its proof of spiritual immaturity and carnality. In whose life is it evident?

    a. 1 Timothy 6:3–5

    b. Titus 3:1–4

    c. Jude 1:15–19

4. Even though fighting and quarreling have been evident in the church since the very beginning, we are called to personally live and "walk in unity." What does God's Word teach us about the importance of unity in the Body of Christ?

JAMES 4:1–6 LESSON #14

   a. John 13:34, 35

   b. Romans 12:16–21

   c. 1Corinthians 1:10

   d. Philippians 2:2, 3

5. James makes it clear that the cause of external fighting and quarreling is truly a war that has its origin in the interior of our hearts. It is a battle that is waged within; a battle that stems from our desire to have or do something to please ourselves regardless of the consequences. As a Christian, how are we to bring peace to this war?

   a. 1Peter 2:1–3

   b. 1Peter 4:2

   c. Colossians 3:7–10

   d. 1John 2:15–17

6. What area of your life has the Lord spoken to you about today? Is there something you need to allow Him to change? Allow Him to mold you into His image today by willingly giving Him your heart and life to use for His glory. Record your prayer here or in a personal journal.

Day 3—Begin in Prayer

1. Read James 4:1–6.

2. Re-read James 4:2, 3.

3. Knowing that the source of the quarrel and fightings within the Body of Christ and in our lives lies deep within our own hearts, we are called to examine those things which drive us. What truly causes us satisfaction and peace? Can it be found in worldly things, the collecting of wealth or the pursuit of pleasure?

    a. Proverbs 15:27

    b. Luke 12:16–21

    c. 1 Timothy 6:9, 10

    d. Ecclesiastes 12:8; 13, 14 (The conclusion of a man who "had it all by the world's standards.")

4. This drive to obtain the pleasures that are sought by the flesh leads to destruction and maybe literal murder. How does the following Scriptural account prove out this destructive nature of the flesh when it is controlled by lust? 2 Samuel 11:1–17.

JAMES 4:1-6   LESSON #14

5. The Bible is repeatedly clear that a driving desire for pleasure, wealth, and power is a hindrance to an effective prayer life. In fact, this lust will cause us to stop praying or to lose the proper perspective of what prayer is meant to be. James tells us that we will forget to ask or we will ask with the wrong motives so that we might "consume it on our own lusts." How must we approach our Heavenly Father in prayer?

    a. 2Chronicles 34:27

    b. Psalm 25:8-12

    c. John 15:7

    d. 1John 5:14

    e. Matthew 21:22

6. What area of your life has the Lord spoken to you about today? Is there something you need to allow Him to change? Allow Him to mold you into His image today by willingly giving Him your heart and life to use for His glory. Record your prayer here or in a personal journal.

| JAMES 4:1-6 | LESSON #14 |

DAY 4—BEGIN IN PRAYER

1. Read James 4:1-6.

2. Re-read James 4:4.

3. James doesn't tread lightly on those who fall into this category of "friends of the world." It doesn't seem possible that a Christian, someone who has trusted in Christ for their salvation, could become "an enemy of God." What strong accusation does James use against this believer and what warnings do we find in the following references that we can use to evaluate our own Christian walk?

   a. Matthew 6:22-24

   b. Matthew 13:22

   c. Luke 12:15

   d. Romans 8:5-8

4. Adultery is a strong term! Friendship with the world means **betrayal** to God. As Christians, we are not to have any **friendship** with the world. We are to be "separate, unspotted and holy." We are to be "in the world but not **of** it." We are called the Bride of Christ, and are to be set apart unto the Lord Jesus Christ. Record the details from the Word of God of this picture of our relationship with the Lord.

   a. Isaiah 54:5

JAMES 4:1-6   LESSON #14

    b. Romans 7:4

    c. 2Corinthians 11:2

    d. Revelation 19:7-9

5. Knowing that we are "The Bride of Christ," how ought we to be living as we await His soon return?

    a. Ephesians 6:13-18

    b. Colossians 4:4, 5

    c. 2Timothy 4:5

    d. 1Peter 4:7, 8

6. What area of your life has the Lord spoken to you about today? Is there something you need to allow Him to change? Allow Him to mold you into His image today by willingly giving Him your heart and life to use for His glory. Record your prayer here or in a personal journal.

JAMES 4:1-6   **136**   LESSON #14

Day 5—Begin in Prayer

1. Read James 4:1-6.

2. Re-read James 4:5, 6.

3. In verse 5, James tells us that our tendency toward friendship with the world causes the Holy Spirit, Who dwells in us, to be jealous over us because of our misplaced loyalty. The Spirit of God wants our love and commitment for Himself exclusively. Understanding that the Holy Spirit's jealousy for us is what is spoken of here, shows us that even when we sin, by seeking our pleasures in friendship with the world, we are greatly loved. How is God's character revealed in the following Scriptures alluded to by James?

    a. Exodus 34:14

    b. Deuteronomy 4:24

    c. 1Kings 14:22

    d. Zechariah 8:2

4. If this tendency of the flesh is toward seeking pleasure from the world and betraying our Heavenly Father Who loves us, how are we to have victory over the flesh? The answer lies in God's abundant, unending resource of grace. God gives greater grace to those who call upon Him. What do we learn about God's grace and how it brings victory to our Christian walk?

    a. Romans 5:1, 2

©2001—Morningstar Christian Chapel, Whittier, CA

JAMES 4:1–6 — LESSON #14

b. 1 Corinthians 15:10

c. 2 Corinthians 9:8

d. 2 Corinthians 12:9, 10

5. Clearly the Scriptures teach us that God resists those who will not submit to His authority; those who declare, by their prideful actions, that they **think** they can have victory over their own sin. Verse 6 reminds us that God's grace is poured out upon the one who comes to God in humility. Record what you learn about God's response to the man who seeks Him in humility.

a. Psalm 34:18

b. Psalm 51:17

c. Isaiah 57:15

d. Isaiah 66:1, 2

6. What area of your life has the Lord spoken to you about today? Is there something you need to allow Him to change? Allow Him to mold you into His image today by willingly giving Him your heart and life to use for His glory. Record your prayer here or in a personal journal.

Day 6—Begin in Prayer

1. Read James 4:1–6.

2. What is the source of the "wars and fighting" within the Body of Christ?

3. Can you outline the path of this lust and its destruction in the believer's life?

4. What awful, descriptive term does God use for His children who align themselves as "friends of the world"?

5. How would you describe yourself: **self-centered, world-centered** or **God-centered**? How would God describe you?

6. "He giveth more grace." Ask Him today to make any needed attitude adjustments in your loyalty. He's waiting! He is jealous for your exclusive love and commitment.

7. Have you completed your memory verse this week? **If not, do so today!**

> Ye adulterers and adulteresses, know ye not that the friendship of the world is enmity with God? Whosoever therefore will be a friend of the world is the enemy of God. James 4:4

JAMES 4:7–10   139   LESSON #15

Day 1 — Begin in Prayer

1. Read James 4:7–10.

2. The solution to the "wars and fighting" that have their source in the depths of our hearts is laid out clearly in these four verses. But, according to verse 6 it only comes to those who willingly come in submission and humility. This is not a battle that we can fight and conquer in our own flesh, filled with pride and self-determination. This battle is won by God's grace through God's power. "But He (God) giveth more grace. Wherefore he saith, God resisteth the proud, but giveth grace unto the humble." We are given a series of nine directives to follow in order to win the war over the flesh, read James 4:7–10 slowly, what are they?

   1.
   2.
   3.
   4.
   5.
   6.
   7.
   8.
   9.

3. Use a dictionary of New Testament Words or Strong's Concordance to define the following words to help give you a better grasp of their meaning.

   a. Submit

   b. Resist

©2001—Morningstar Christian Chapel, Whittier, CA

c. Draw near

d. Humble

4. Choose a verse to memorize this week. **(May I suggest James 4:7–10?)** We need this direction engraved on our hearts. Begin working on it today.

Day 2—Begin in Prayer

1. Read James 4:7–10.

2. Re-read James 4:7.

3. James teaches us that victory over the flesh comes through the act of submitting to God. The word **submit (hypotasso)** means: **to get in proper rank behind the leader.** The truth is, no believer came to the Lord unbowed. James calls us back to this initial submissiveness. It is to be our everyday experience. What reminder of this truth do we find in the following Biblical accounts of humble submission?

    a. 2Chronicles 30:8, 9

    b. 2Chronicles 33:12, 13

    c. Daniel 4:29–37

JAMES 4:7–10   LESSON #15

   d. Luke 15:11–24

4. We are instructed "to resist **(to set one's self against; to withstand; to oppose)** the devil." How are we to do so?

   a. Matthew 4:1–11

   b. Ephesians 6:11–18

   c. Luke 10:17–19

5. How can we practice this action of "resisting the devil" in our everyday life?

   a. Romans 13:11–14

   b. 2Corinthians 2:9–11

   c. Ephesians 4:24–31

   d. 1Peter 5:8, 9

What promises are given to those who "resist the devil"?

6. What area of your life has the Lord spoken to you about today? Is there something you need to allow Him to change? Allow Him to mold you into His image today by willingly giving Him your heart and life to use for His glory. Record your prayer here or in a personal journal.

Day 3—Begin in Prayer

1. Read James 4:7–10.

2. Re-read James 4:8.

3. James gives us instructions to **draw near to God**. What will happen to our view of ourselves as we draw closer to the Lord?

   a. Isaiah 6:1–8

   b. Job 42:1–6

   c. Luke 5:8

Give some examples of actions, thoughts, or beliefs that might hinder us from drawing near to God.

JAMES 4:7–10 — LESSON #15

4. We are commanded to "cleanse our hands and purify our hearts." How does the believer accomplish this daily?

   a. Psalm 19:12–14

   b. Psalm 51:1–10

   c. Ephesians 5:25b–27

   d. 1John 1:7–9

5. What does James 1:8 tell us about the "double-minded man"?

The Lord calls us to a single-minded allegiance to Himself. He wants us to have eyes only for Him! Our eyes and hearts are to seek Him and His ways, not pulled and wandering because of an allegiance to the world. What does God's Word teach us about our need for a single-minded love for the Lord Jesus Christ?

   a. Matthew 5:8

   b. Matthew 6:22–24

JAMES 4:7–10 — LESSON #15

    c. Colossians 3:1–4

    d. 1John 2:15–17

6. What area of your life has the Lord spoken to you about today? Is there something you need to allow Him to change? Allow Him to mold you into His image today by willingly giving Him your heart and life to use for His glory. Record your prayer here or in a personal journal.

Day 4—Begin in Prayer

1. Read James 4:7–10.

2. Re-read James 4:9.

3. James is not calling for the believer to live a life of gloom and sadness, but we must be careful to recognize that sin separates us from intimate fellowship with our Heavenly Father. He is holy and cannot tolerate sin. Use the following Scriptures as a reminder of the perfection of God's holy character.

    a. Leviticus 11:45

    b. Joshua 24:19–24

    c. Psalm 99:9

JAMES 4:7-10 — LESSON #15

d. 1Peter 1:14-16

4. Do you remember Isaiah's recognition of his sinfulness? Is this your assessment when you examine your life? Godly sorrow precedes true repentance. What does 2Corinthians 7:8-10 teach us about repentance?

Compare the repentance of Judas (Matthew 27:3-5) with that of Peter (Luke 22:61, 62; 24:12).

Personal: Godly repentance is defined as: sorry enough to stop and seek for God's help and forgiveness. Does sin grieve your heart? Are you sorry enough to humble yourself before God and stop? "He giveth more grace" and it is by His strength that you will be able to have victory.

5. God calls **us** to be holy as we learned in 1Peter 1:16. What more do we learn about this high calling and how God desires to accomplish His work in our lives?

a. Romans 12:1-3

b. Philippians 2:12, 13

c. Philippians 4:13

JAMES 4:7–10	LESSON #15

d. 1Peter 2:9–12

6. What area of your life has the Lord spoken to you about today? Is there something you need to allow Him to change? Allow Him to mold you into His image today by willingly giving Him your heart and life to use for His glory. Record your prayer here or in a personal journal.

DAY 5—BEGIN IN PRAYER

1. Read James 4:7–10.

2. Re-read James 4:10.

3. Finally, James gives us the summary command of the method by which we are to have victory over the flesh, ending the wars and fighting's among us. The answer is to "humble ourselves." When we do, He will show Himself strong on our behalf and "He will lift us up." God evidently wants us to get the point. Jesus repeated this truth on three separate occasions. Record them and, as you do, pray that God will work this humility into your everyday walk.

   a. Luke 18:14

   b. Matthew 23:12

   c. Luke 14:11

4. To **humble** means to **make low; bring low; to abase; to assign a lower rank or place to; of one's soul bring down one's pride; to have a modest opinion of one's self.** We are to make ourselves low in the sight of God,

JAMES 4:7–10 — LESSON #15

seeing ourselves for who we are according to the Lord's standard, and trust Him to do His work in and through us. If we want to be up, we must go down! What further encouragement do you receive from the following Scriptures about this eternal truth?

a. 2Kings 22:19, 20

b. Isaiah 57:15

c. Proverbs 29:23

d. Micah 6:8

e. 1Peter 5:6, 7

5. When we do humble ourselves before God, He gives us **greater** grace (v. 6). **Greater then what? Greater** than the draw of the world; **greater** than the lust of the flesh; **greater** than the temptation of the enemy. If we want victory, we must surrender our will to His. What was the Lord's answer to Paul regarding his thorn in the flesh in 2Corinthians 12:8, 9?

Personal: The same truth and promise is available today to the humble seeker!

6. What area of your life has the Lord spoken to you about today? Is there something you need to allow Him to change? Allow Him to mold you into His image today by willingly giving Him your heart and life to use for His glory. Record your prayer here or in a personal journal.

DAY 6—BEGIN IN PRAYER

1. Read James 4:7–10.

2. Record the nine directives given as the answers for victory in the Christian walk **again**.

    1.

    2.

    3.

    4.

    5.

    6.

    7.

    8.

    9.

    Begin to make these actions a habit in your life! You will see God's grace abound in your life like never before.

3. Have you completed your memory verse(s) this week? **If not, do so today!**

Submit yourselves therefore to God. Resist the devil, and he will flee from you. Draw nigh to God, and He will draw nigh to you. Cleanse your hands, ye sinners; and purify your hearts, ye double minded. Be afflicted, and mourn, and weep: let your laughter be turned to mourning, and your joy to heaviness. Humble yourselves in the sight of the Lord, and He shall lift you up. James 4:7–10

150

JAMES 4:11-17 — LESSON #16

DAY 1—BEGIN IN PRAYER

1. Read James 4:11-17.

2. What is the main subject of the two following paragraphs in this portion of James?

    a. James 4:11, 12

    b. James 4:13-17

3. What word in verse 11 reminds us that James is talking about the sin of the believer speaking evil against his brother or sister in Christ?

4. James asks two probing questions in this portion of His letter. What are they?

    a.

    b.

5. Choose a verse to memorize this week. Begin working on it now.

DAY 2—BEGIN IN PRAYER

1. Read James 4:11-17.

2. Re-read James 4:11, 12.

3. To **speak evil** means: **to talk against; to find fault with; to defame or slander.** But, this command in Greek carries a broader meaning: **do not say untrue, malicious things.** It says that we should never say anything that would negatively affect another person, even if it is **true**. The command is **do not speak evil of one another!** No excuses, no exceptions, and no good reason! What further reminder and direction do we get regarding our speech among the brethren?

   a. Psalm 34:13-15

   b. Ephesians 4:31, 32

   c. 1Peter 2:1, 2

   d. 1Peter 3:10-12

4. As believers, we are called to discernment and judgment of actions. We are not to allow sin to be practiced in the lives of those who trust Jesus as their Lord and Savior. We are to judge actions, but not motives or intent of the heart. The evil words and judgment that James is condemning is that which is motivated by pride and wishes to destroy; not build up, heal and restore. James warns us against this sin of having a critical, judgmental spirit. What do we learn from this picture in Matthew 7:1-5 that clearly illustrates the lesson of James 4:11?

JAMES 4:11-17 — LESSON #16

5. Judgment of man's heart and motives means placing one's self above the law and above the Lawgiver Himself. Who is the only Judge and how does being reminded of this help you to speak more carefully of your brothers and sisters in the Lord?

   a. Isaiah 33:22

   b. Romans 14:4

   c. Romans 14:10-12

   d. 1Corinthians 4:3-5

6. What area of your life has the Lord spoken to you about today? Is there something you need to allow Him to change? Allow Him to mold you into His image today by willingly giving Him your heart and life to use for His glory. Record your prayer here or in a personal journal.

DAY 3—BEGIN IN PRAYER

1. Read James 4:11-17.

2. Re-read James 4:13, 14.

3. Not only were some in James' church disregarding the Lord by passing judgment upon their brethren, many were making plans to live, do business and prosper while ignoring the providence of God. They were calling themselves followers of the Lord Jesus Christ but never seeking His guidance or direction for their plans. What do the Scriptures say about your life and Who is in control of it?

a. Proverbs 16:9

b. Psalms 37:23, 24

c. Isaiah 46:9–11

d. Jeremiah 10:23

e. Lamentations 3:37

4. The Lord is not against His children planning for the future, but He is against man's self-serving, self-dependent claim to a knowledge of the future and a disregard of His will. Describe the attitude of the man described in Luke 12:17–20. Can you give a modern day illustration?

   What ought our attitude be toward the things of this world, even the things we need to live? See Luke 12:22–31.

5. James declares, how arrogant of you to think that tomorrow is guaranteed to you! Your life is like "a vapor"! Here for a moment and then gone. This being true, how ought we to live today?

JAMES 4:11–17 — LESSON #16

a. Psalm 39:4, 5

b. Psalm 90:12

c. Luke 12:35–38

d. Ephesians 5:15–17

6. What area of your life has the Lord spoken to you about today? Is there something you need to allow Him to change? Allow Him to mold you into His image today by willingly giving Him your heart and life to use for His glory. Record your prayer here or in a personal journal.

DAY 4—BEGIN IN PRAYER

1. Read James 4:11–17.

2. Re-read James 4:15, 16.

3. James has shown us the error in planning arrogantly for tomorrow, or next year, without reference to God's will. He tells us in verse 15 what we ought to be saying, and more importantly, what principle of submission **must** rule our lives. How was this heart of submission exhibited in the lives of the disciples?

a. Acts 18:21

b. 1Corinthians 4:19

c. Hebrews 6:3

Personal: Are these words and this attitude written over your daily calendar or "to do" list?

4. Paul did not consider the will of God to be a chain that shackled him; rather, it was a key that opened doors and set him free. We should not fear the will of God, because of His love for us, it is the best and safest place we can be. Finding God's will for your life is a growing experience and if we are willing to obey, He is willing to reveal. Record John 7:17.

What are some general truths that are the will of God? Are you doing these? As you do, God will give you more specific direction.

   a. 1Thessalonians 4:3, 4

   b. 1Thessalonians 5:16–18

   c. 1Peter 2:15, 16

   d. 1Peter 4:19

JAMES 4:11–17 — LESSON #16

5. Not only were these prideful believers making plans as if they had control over their future, they were **boasting (to speak loudly; to be loud-tongued; to vaunt one's self)** in their success. James says all such haughty pride is evil, bad, useless, and good for nothing. There is an added meaning in Greek which says: **this boasting is toilsome, painful, and grievous—to the boaster, his audience, and most of all to the heart of God.** Rather than boasting in our own accomplishments, what should we boast in?

   a. Psalm 34:2

   b. Psalm 44:8

   c. Jeremiah 9:23, 24

   d. 1Corinthians 1:27–31

6. What area of your life has the Lord spoken to you about today? Is there something you need to allow Him to change? Allow Him to mold you into His image today by willingly giving Him your heart and life to use for His glory. Record your prayer here or in a personal journal.

DAY 5—BEGIN IN PRAYER

1. Read James 4:11–17.

2. Re-read James 4:17.

3. It is true that with knowledge comes responsibility. James lays it on the line. If you know to do good, and you do not do it, **it is sin!** Review chapter 4, what good do we now know to do?

4. Sin is not only **the act of doing something wrong**. It is also sin when we do not do **something that is right**. The believers in James' church knew what God's will was for them and, therefore, if they refused to obey they were judged guilty. Record the main details of this parable of Jesus in Luke 12:41–48.

   What did the wise servant do? What was his reward?

   What was the attitude of the unwise servant? What was his punishment?

   What is the conclusion of this matter and what is our responsibility to faithfully obey what we know is right to do (v. 48b)?

5. These merchants had traveled, without consulting their Heavenly Father and prospered by His merciful hand, but refused to acknowledge His blessing. Then they returned home in bragging, boastful pride. What is the good news for us, as believers, when we have been caught in a trap baited by our flesh and the enemy?

   a. 2Chronicles 7:14

   b. Psalms 32:5

   c. Proverbs 28:13

JAMES 4:11–17 — LESSON #16

d. 1 John 1:9

6. What area of your life has the Lord spoken to you about today? Is there something you need to allow Him to change? Allow Him to mold you into His image today by willingly giving Him your heart and life to use for His glory. Record your prayer here or in a personal journal.

DAY 6—BEGIN IN PRAYER

1. Read James 4:11–17.

2. In as few words as possible, summarize the message of each of the following verses.

   a. Verse 11

   b. Verse 12

   c. Verses 13, 14

   d. Verse 15

   e. Verse 16

   f. Verse 17

3. As Christians, what counsel are we to trust when it comes to tomorrow regarding our concern and worry for those things that we will need? (Matthew 6:34)

Personal: Only One is the Judge! Has learning this truth helped control your speech? Did your heart's attitude and prayer this morning include God in your plans? Remember, when you know to do good, and do not do it, it is sin. Ask the Lord in prayer to enable you to trust Him, to submit to His will, and obey Him. He's waiting to be all that you need.

4. Did you complete your memory verse this week? **If not, do so today**.

For that ye ought to say, If the Lord will, we shall live, and do this, or that. James 4:15

JAMES 5:1-6 LESSON #17

DAY 1—BEGIN IN PRAYER

1. Read James 5:1-6.

2. In this section of James, we are warned of the plight of the wicked rich. They have stock-piled goods, cheated their workers, and gluttonously lived their lives. The warning is crystal clear—it's only **temporary** and judgment **will** come. Summarize the three parts of this warning in your own words.

   a. Verses 1-3

   b. Verse 4

   c. Verses 5, 6

3. James' strong words of exhortation seem to be directed at the rich, unbelieving farmers and landowners who were oppressing and exploiting the poor of the church. Contrast the salutation in verse 1 with that in verse 7. What do you notice about the difference?

4. Meditate on the sure truth of Proverbs 15:27. What are you using all your energy chasing after?

5. Choose a verse to memorize this week. Begin working on it today.

DAY 2—BEGIN IN PRAYER

1. Read James 5:1-6.

JAMES 5:1–6   LESSON #17

2. Re-read James 5:1.

3. James is contrasting the world's value system with the one God truly desires to be the focus of our lives. In the materialistic society in which we live, we are bombarded by the lie that **stuff** satisfies. It has not, cannot and **never will satisfy**. As believers, how will our every need be satisfied?

   a. Psalm 16:11

   b. Psalm 17:15

   c. Acts 2:25–28

   d. Matthew 5:6

4. The problem of oppression and mistreatment of the poor is not new to our generation. It occurred in the early church, in David's time, and in the beginning of history. The companion problem of envy and jealousy is a temptation that is faced by everyone. Read Psalm 73. What problem did the Psalmist face? What was the solution? How can you apply this lesson to any envy or jealousy in your life today?

5. Our Heavenly Father is less concerned about the actual amount of wealth than He is about our heart's attitude, which directs its accumulation, its use and its desire for more. We must check our priorities, guard our principles, and value what is eternal. What do we learn about the correct relationship between a Christian and the material things of this world from 1 Timothy 6:7-19? Record a **few major points** that are particularly significant to you.

6. What area of your life has the Lord spoken to you about today? Is there something you need to allow Him to change? Allow Him to mold you into His image today by willingly giving Him your heart and life to use for His glory. Record your prayer here or in a personal journal.

Day 3—Begin in Prayer

1. Read James 5:1-6.

2. Re-read James 5:2, 3.

3. These wicked rich men that James addresses were amassing "treasures" that would not last. How does James vividly describe each of the following **worldly treasures**?

    a. Riches

    b. Garments

    c. Gold and Silver

Personal: Do you consider any of the above to be of high-priority in your life? Review their true value. Ask the Lord to help you put first things first and correctly align your priorities.

4. These wicked men were heaping "treasure together for the last days," although it would be the very thing that would testify against them in judgment. Rather than "treasure" that will burn in the fire of God's judgment, what **eternal treasure** are we to be investing our lives in?

   a. Isaiah 33:5, 6

   b. Matthew 6:19-21

   c. Matthew 19:16-22

   d. Hebrews 10:34-36

   What, specifically, would be a **treasure in heaven?**

5. Remember the man that thought he **had it all?** Review the parable that Jesus taught in Luke 12:16-21. What surprise came to this man? Where were his riches stored?

JAMES 5:1–6   LESSON #17

Write out the warning Jesus gave to you and me just before He taught this parable. Luke 12:15. Selah!

6. What area of your life has the Lord spoken to you about today? Is there something you need to allow Him to change? Allow Him to mold you into His image today by willingly giving Him your heart and life to use for His glory. Record your prayer here or in a personal journal.

Day 4—Begin in Prayer

1. Read James 5:1–6.

2. Re-read James 5:4.

3. These wealthy rich landowners gained their riches by deceitful, fraudulent means. God saw their evil actions and heard the cries of those whom they oppressed. What do we learn about God's command regarding being an honest, fair steward and employer before the Lord?

    a. Leviticus 19:13

    b. Deuteronomy 24:14, 15

    c. Jeremiah 22:13, 14

    d. Colossians 4:1

JAMES 5:1-6 — LESSON #17

4. We can stand assured that **the cries of the oppressed are heard on High** and judgment **will** come. Use the following Scripture references to evaluate your business dealings and to be encouraged if you are in the midst of a trial in which you are being mistreated.

   a. Exodus 22:22, 23

   b. Malachi 3:5

   c. Hebrews 10:30, 31

   d. Jude 1:14, 15

5. James uses a Name of God that is frequently used throughout the Old Testament. (Mentioned 269 times.) It shows us His character and nature. The LORD of Hosts is the avenger of the poor, the needy and the oppressed. He hears their cries and comes in judgment. What more do we learn about Jehovah Sabaoth from the following references?

   a. 1 Samuel 17:45, 46

   b. Psalm 46:7

   c. Isaiah 6:1-3

JAMES 5:1–6   LESSON #17

d. Isaiah 9:6, 7

e. Zechariah 4:6

6. What area of your life has the Lord spoken to you about today? Is there something you need to allow Him to change? Allow Him to mold you into His image today by willingly giving Him your heart and life to use for His glory. Record your prayer here or in a personal journal.

DAY 5—BEGIN IN PRAYER

1. Read James 5:1–6.

2. Re-read James 5:5, 6.

3. Use a Dictionary of New Testament Words or Strong's Concordance to define the following words to give you a better understanding of their meaning:

   a. Pleasure

   b. Wanton

   c. Nourished

   d. Slaughter

4. How is such a self-indulgent lifestyle evident in our world today?

As Christians, we are to be faithful stewards and vessels of God's provision. What do the following Scriptures teach us about helping to meet others' needs?

a. Matthew 5:42

b. Acts 20:35

c. 2Corinthians 9:7-12

d. Ephesians 4:28

5. James even indicts these wicked men for murder. "Ye have killed"—maybe it wasn't a physical murder but it was certainly possible. It is easy for the poor and powerless to be eliminated. It can happen through no access to "true justice" within the court system, because of lack of money, or by being driven to hopelessness by rejection. However, the cry of the oppressed shall be heard and justice will be administered. How ought we to live that will stand as a testimony against the ungodly wicked of this world?

a. Psalm 1:1-3

b. Psalm 24:3-5

JAMES 5:1-6 — LESSON #17

c. Isaiah 33:15, 16

6. What area of your life has the Lord spoken to you about today? Is there something you need to allow Him to change? Allow Him to mold you into His image today by willingly giving Him your heart and life to use for His glory. Record your prayer here or in a personal journal.

DAY 6—BEGIN IN PRAYER

1. Read James 5:1-6.

2. Read Psalm 26, slowly and prayerfully. How does it minister to your heart today? Does the word **integrity** describe your dealings with your spouse, children, employees, employers, family and neighbors?

   Spend time in prayer asking the Lord to make verse 11 the prayer of your heart and life.

3. Have you completed your memory verse this week? **If not, do so today.**

   Go to now, ye rich men, weep and howl for your miseries that shall come upon you. James 5:1

170

DAY 1 — BEGIN IN PRAYER

1. Read James 5:7–12.

2. How are these verses a great comfort to those who were suffering under the cruel oppression of the wicked landowners in the previous verses 1–6? How are they a comfort to you as a believer in a society that increasingly rejects your Lord and Savior Jesus Christ and your faith?

3. Record the three exhortations concerning the coming of the Lord found in these verses?

4. Record the definitions of the following words and use what you learn as a prayer before the Lord to encourage patient, expectant waiting in your heart and life.

    a. Patient (v. 7)

    b. Stablish (Establish) (v. 8)

5. Choose a verse to memorize this week. Begin working on it today.

DAY 2 — BEGIN IN PRAYER

1. Read James 5:7–12.

2. Re-read James 5:7, 8.

3. James tells us of our need to be patient through the midst of suffering, but this is not a mere suggestion. This exhortation is written in the form of a command. We are not to wait passively, but to live in active expectancy of our Lord's soon return. What further encouragement can we gain from the following Scriptures that will help in our patient waiting?

   a. Psalm 130:5-7

   b. Lamentations 3:25, 26

   c. Hebrews 10:35-37

   d. Revelation 22:20

4. To be certain that we understand the necessity of patient waiting, James gives us a very vivid illustration. "The husbandman (the farmer) patiently waits for the precious fruit of the earth." He needs the early and latter rain. Fall rains softened the soil for planting and germination. Winter and Spring rains provided the nourishment that helped to produce an abundant harvest. The farmer has no control over the weather, nor any other circumstance, that causes mature crop growth. He **must patiently wait** and **trust** the One Who created the earth and rules over nature. Likewise we, who wait eagerly for the Lord's soon return, must trust Him with our lives and the circumstances which we face daily. What do you learn about His care for your life?

   a. Psalm 33:11

   b. Isaiah 43:1-3

c. Isaiah 46:9-11

d. 2Corinthians 12:8-10

5. We are called to "establish **(to make stable; place firmly; set fast; fix; to strengthen)** our hearts." What means does God use to help us "establish our hearts"?

   a. Psalms 27:14

   b. Psalm 40:1-3

   c. Romans 1:11, 12

   d. Galatians 5:22-25

6. What area of your life has the Lord spoken to you about today? Is there something you need to allow Him to change? Allow Him to mold you into His image today by willingly giving Him your heart and life to use for His glory. Record your prayer here or in a personal journal.

JAMES 5:7–12 — LESSON #18

DAY 3—BEGIN IN PRAYER

1. Read James 5:7–12.

2. Re-read James 5:9.

3. Why do you think that James would need to add this direction regarding grudging one another in the middle of his exhortation to patiently endure hardship and persecution?

4. The Lord gives us a very clear warning through James. We are not to grudge one another. We are not to pass judgment on them concerning their motives, their lives or God's dealing with them. Why?

How does the knowledge that the Lord, the Judge, stands at the door and hears your every word, make a difference in what you think or say? See Matthew 12:35–37.

Refresh your memory regarding James' earlier direction regarding the words we speak. Ask the Lord to reign over your tongue today!

a. James 1:26

b. James 2:8

c. James 2:12

JAMES 5:7-12 — LESSON #18

d. James 4:11, 12

5. As children of the Lord, who believe that God is in control and that nothing touches our lives that He does not allow, how should our words and attitudes be characterized?

   a. Hebrews 13:15

   b. Ephesians 4:29-32

   c. Ephesians 5:3, 4

   d. Colossians 4:5, 6

6. What area of your life has the Lord spoken to you about today? Is there something you need to allow Him to change? Allow Him to mold you into His image today by willingly giving Him your heart and life to use for His glory. Record your prayer here or in a personal journal.

DAY 4—BEGIN IN PRAYER

1. Read James 5:7-12.

2. Re-read James 5:10, 11.

3. James lays out some true life examples of those who patiently suffered. He says, take the prophets for instance and by James' day there had been so many that he didn't attempt a list. Read over the following accounts of one day in the life of a couple of prophets, what do you think of their patient example of suffering affliction?

   a. Jeremiah – Jeremiah 38:1-13

   b. Micaiah – 1Kings 22:24-27

   c. Elijah – 1Kings 18:21-40

   d. Daniel – Daniel 6:11-23

4. Then there is the life story of Job! James says you have heard of "the patience of Job." Record a few details of the inside information we have regarding Job's life that were unknown to this man of faith. Job 1:1-19

   What was Job's response? Job 1:20-22

   The enemies further accusations? Job 2:1-6

JAMES 5:7–12 — LESSON #18

Was Job's faith proven and purified through this time of testing? (Job 42:1–6.) Record verses 5 and 6. Describe how Job's faith had changed and matured through patiently enduring through affliction.

5. James proclaims, "we count them happy which endure." True faith demands a life-long commitment in spite of the circumstances; in spite of the people; in spite of the hardship. We count them blessed that endure. What more do we learn from the following verses about the characteristic of perseverance through to the end?

   a. Matthew 10:21, 22

   b. Hebrews 3:14

   c. James 1:12

   d. 1Peter 1:6, 7

6. What area of your life has the Lord spoken to you about today? Is there something you need to allow Him to change? Allow Him to mold you into His image today by willingly giving Him your heart and life to use for His glory. Record your prayer here or in a personal journal.

JAMES 5:7–12 — LESSON #18

DAY 5—BEGIN IN PRAYER

1. Read James 5:7–12.

2. Re-read James 5:12.

3. The practice of swearing an oath or taking a vow is discussed by James in light of our need to wait patiently for the Lord's soon return. It was a practice encouraged in the Old Testament days and the taking of oaths or making vows was considered binding and an individual was expected to keep his word. Gather some Old Testament background on oaths and swearing.

   a. Leviticus 19:12

   b. Numbers 30:2

   c. Deuteronomy 10:20

   d. Jeremiah 12:16

4. It was the common practice in Jesus' and James' day to make oaths. However, by this time people used the practice to lie, cheat, and steal. Therefore, Jesus gave clear direction about the truthfulness of the speech of the believer and how it ought to show forth the character of the new heart. What did Jesus teach about the practice of swearing and vowing?

   a. Matthew 5:33–37

JAMES 5:7-12   LESSON #18

    b. Matthew 23:16-22

5. Finally, in dealing with **waiting** we are to watch what we say and how we say it. When our patience fails, it is most often demonstrated by the words that flow from our mouths. With this exhortative reminder that the Judge stands before the door, make Psalm 141:3 the prayer of your heart today as you patiently "establish your heart for the coming of the Lord."

6. What area of your life has the Lord spoken to you about today? Is there something you need to allow Him to change? Allow Him to mold you into His image today by willingly giving Him your heart and life to use for His glory. Record your prayer here or in a personal journal.

DAY 6—BEGIN IN PRAYER

1. Read James 5:7-12.

2. How are we to be like the farmer?

    How are we to be like the prophets?

    How are we to be like Job?

3. How ought this patient waiting affect our relationship with others?

How ought this patient waiting affect our speech?

How are you doing? Patient and established or impatient and grudgingly swearing? Ask the Lord to pinpoint the areas you need Him to establish and strengthen.

4. Have you completed your memory verse for this week? **If not, do so today.**

> Be patient therefore, brethren, unto the coming of the Lord. Behold, the husbandman waiteth for the precious fruit of the earth, and hath long patience for it, until he receive the early and latter rain. Be ye also patient; stablish your hearts: for the coming of the Lord draweth nigh. James 5:7, 8

JAMES 5:13-20   181   LESSON #19

DAY 1—BEGIN IN PRAYER

1. Read James 5:13-20.

2. What would you say is the main topic of this final section in James' letter?

3. Record a few of the details you learn about how and when to pray?

4. Use your Dictionary of New Testament Words, Strong's Concordance or an English Language Dictionary to find the deeper meaning of the following words:

   a. Afflicted (v. 13)

   b. Sick (v. 14)

   c. Faults (v. 16)

   d. Convert (v. 19)

5. Choose a verse to memorize this week. Begin working on it today.

JAMES 5:13–20　　　　**182**　　　　LESSON #19

Day 2—Begin in Prayer

1. Read James 5:13–20.

2. Re-read James 5:13.

3. We are being told as a statement of fact (in original text punctuation marks were not given) that there are those among us who are **afflicted (facing adversity; hardship; trouble from without)**. When trouble besieges our life, we are to: **pray (Greek = proseuchomai; turn toward God)**. What do we learn about our access to our Heavenly Father because of our relationship with His Son, Jesus Christ?

    a. Romans 8:15–17

    b. Hebrews 4:15, 16

    c. Ephesians 2:18, 19

    d. 1Peter 2:9, 10

4. Therefore, we are to pray in our affliction. What are we to seek God for?

    What comfort and encouragement do you find from these Scriptures to strengthen you in the midst of affliction?

    a. Psalm 34:17–19

b. John 16:33

c. 2Corinthians 4:7-11

d. 1Peter 5:10

5. We get very clear direction to follow in times when life is going well, when we are merry. It would seem obvious, but it is not always the case, because often in times of prosperity and joy we tend to forget our need for the Lord. When we are joyful and merry we are to sing psalms of praise to our Heavenly Father. Record the exhortation to praise found in the following Scriptures.

   a. Psalm 9:2

   b. Psalm 105:2, 3

   c. Ephesians 5:18-20

   d. Colossians 3:16, 17

Personal: Are you afflicted? Are you praying? Are you merry? Are you praising? It is possible to do both at the same time. See Acts 16:23-25.

6. What area of your life has the Lord spoken to you about today? Is there something you need to allow Him to change? Allow Him to mold you into His image today by willingly giving Him your heart and life to use for His glory. Record your prayer here or in a personal journal.

DAY 3—BEGIN IN PRAYER

1. Read James 5:13–20.

2. Re-read James 5:14, 15.

3. James continues: you have afflicted among you, you have merry among you and you do have **sick (to be weak; feeble; to be without strength; powerless)** among you and it is wrong to declare otherwise. There is no Biblical basis for believing that a Christian will not, at times, be sick, even with a terminal sickness that leads to death.

    a. What is this believer to do when he/she suffers from sickness?

    b. What are the elders to do?

    c. Who does the healing?

4. It is clear from the Scriptures that God **can** and **does** heal spiritually and physically. From the following accounts of Jesus' healing ministry, record a few details of each incident. What can we learn about how and when Jesus heals?

    a. Mark 5:25–34

JAMES 5:13-20 — LESSON #19

b. Mark 7:31-35

c. Mark 8:22-25

d. John 4:46-50

e. John 9:6, 7

f. John 11:41-44

Note: What we can learn is that God heals according to His perfect plan, in His perfect time, and according to His perfect will. We cannot demand His action, nor formalize His ways. He is Sovereign and has a perfect plan for our lives even when it includes affliction and sickness as tools to bring us closer to Him. Our faith must be in Him alone knowing that He will accomplish His will in our life.

5. The oil is symbolic of the power of the Holy Spirit. It represents the truth that God's work is not accomplished through man's strength. It is not the oil that heals, or even the prayer of the elders. The healing is accomplished by the Lord. The elders are to pray in the Name of the Lord. Praying in His Name focuses our prayer on our **inability** and God's **ability.** To pray in Jesus' Name means to pray according to His will. What do we learn about the correct condition of the heart of the one who seeks God in prayer?

a. John 14:13

JAMES 5:13-20 LESSON #19

b. John 15:7

c. 1John 3:22

d. 1John 5:14, 15

6. What area of your life has the Lord spoken to you about today? Is there something you need to allow Him to change? Allow Him to mold you into His image today by willingly giving Him your heart and life to use for His glory. Record your prayer here or in a personal journal.

DAY 4—BEGIN IN PRAYER

1. Read James 5:13-20.

2. Re-read James 5:16-18.

3. In this area of prayer James gives us a clear directive that will cause us to build up and encourage one another, as well as, be accountable in our lives and actions to others. We need to **cautiously** be willing to honestly share our faults and shortcomings with others in order to have them pray for strength, power and victory in our lives. What do these Scriptures tell us about our need to support each other?

a. Proverbs 27:17

b. Ecclesiastes 4:9-12

©2001—MORNINGSTAR CHRISTIAN CHAPEL, WHITTIER, CA

c. Hebrews 10:24, 25

d. Colossians 1:9-11

4. James 5:16b says: "the effectual fervent prayer of a righteous man avails much." Who is a "righteous man"?

   a. Romans 5:18, 19

   b. Romans 8:1-4

   c. 2Corinthians 5:21

   d. 1Peter 2:24, 25

5. James gives us an Old Testament example of a faithful man of prayer. Elijah was held in high esteem by the Jews of James' day, almost as if he were super-human. He tells us "Elijah was a man subject to like passions," as they were (and we are). "He prayed earnestly," and it didn't rain for three and a half years. Then, "he prayed again and it rained." Study this part of Elijah's life and his encounter with the prophets of Baal in 1Kings 17-18. Record a few details to help remind you of his faithfulness.

JAMES 5:13–20   **LESSON #19**

Now, remember Elijah was a man of "like passions;" a man just like us. What did this man of prayer do in 1Kings 19?

How does this encourage us to be more faithful in prayer for those who are afflicted and sick among the Body of Christ?

6. What area of your life has the Lord spoken to you about today? Is there something you need to allow Him to change? Allow Him to mold you into His image today by willingly giving Him your heart and life to use for His glory. Record your prayer here or in a personal journal.

DAY 5—BEGIN IN PRAYER

1. Read James 5:13–20.

2. Re-read James 5:19, 20.

3. James addresses one more vital area as he quickly ends his letter: that of the necessity of rescuing wayward believers. Notice, carefully, that he is speaking to the **brethren** and speaking of **any of you**. The NKJV translates this phrase, "if anyone **among you** wanders from the truth." Those who have wandered away from the truth we are to pursue in prayer and action as the Lord leads. What direction are we given in the following verses?

    a. Isaiah 35:3, 4

    b. Luke 22:32

©2001—MORNINGSTAR CHRISTIAN CHAPEL, WHITTIER, CA

JAMES 5:13-20   LESSON #19

    c. Romans 15:1, 2

    d. Galatians 6:1, 2

4. The word "convert" means to **bring the straying one back**. What two things does James want the rescuer to know?

In the context of this verse (see James 5:15) what kind of "death" is verse 20 speaking about?

5. James illustrates love in action in these last few verses of his letter. The work of saving souls and covering sin is God's work. It is a blessing that He desires to use us as vessels to accomplish His work. Use the following Scriptures to guide you as you reach out to help restore those who have "erred from the truth."

    a. Daniel 12:3

    b. Proverbs 11:30

    c. John 15:13

    d. 2Timothy 2:24, 25

6. What area of your life has the Lord spoken to you about today? Is there something you need to allow Him to change? Allow Him to mold you into His image today by willingly giving Him your heart and life to use for His glory. Record your prayer here or in a personal journal.

DAY 6—BEGIN IN PRAYER (Remember the Holy Spirit is your teacher!)

1. Read James 5:13–20.

2. Are you afflicted? What should you be doing?

   Are you merry? What should you be doing?

   Are you gravely ill? What action are you to take?

3. How open have you been in seeking prayer for your failures and weaknesses and being fervent in praying for others? The Lord used Elijah and He wants to use your life. **Will you seek Him fervently in prayer?**

4. Do you know someone that has erred from the truth, what would the Lord have **you** to do, **in love?**

5. Have you completed your memory verse this week? There will be a test!

   > Confess your faults one to another, and pray one for another, that ye may be healed. The effectual fervent prayer of a righteous man availeth much. James 5:16

JAMES 1–5 REVIEW — LESSON #20

Now that we have completed our study of James, let's take a week to reflect on all that we have learned, allowing the Lord access to the very depths of our hearts to make any necessary changes that He desires. Spend time in prayer surrendering your will to His heart. Record your prayer here!

DAY 1—BEGIN IN PRAYER

1. Read James 1.

2. To whom is this letter written? Who wrote it?

3. What are the major points contained in this chapter?

4. What encouragement do you receive?

5. What promises do you find?

6. What warnings are written that we must heed?

7. How has studying this chapter helped you when facing trials? How has your understanding of trials changed in this last year?

DAY 2—BEGIN IN PRAYER

1. Read James 2.

2. What are the major points contained in this chapter?

3. What encouragement do you receive?

4. What promises do you find?

JAMES 1–5 REVIEW — LESSON #20

5. What warnings are written that we must heed?

6. What conclusion is drawn regarding the **profession of faith without the evidence of action?**

7. How has your judgment of others been changed through James' teaching? What do you understand to be true regarding faith without works?

Personal: Is your faith obvious to all who are watching your life?

Day 3—Begin in Prayer

1. Read James 3.

2. What are the major points contained in this chapter?

JAMES 1–5 REVIEW

LESSON #20

3. What encouragement do you receive?

4. What promises do you find?

5. What warnings are written that we must heed?

6. How can we tame this little member of our body? How do our words reflect the contents of our heart?

7. How has detailed study of the tongue and its potential for awesome goodness, or destructive evil, helped you personally? **Does God have the reigns of your tongue?**

JAMES 1–5 REVIEW — LESSON #20

DAY 4—BEGIN IN PRAYER

1. Read James 4.

2. What are the major points contained in this chapter?

3. What encouragement do you receive?

4. What promises do you find?

5. What warnings are written that we must heed?

6. What is the source of the fighting and wars among us? How does the Word describe **friendship with the world**?

JAMES 1–5 REVIEW — LESSON #20

7. How is it that we can have victory over the flesh? Record the process of submission to the Lord detailed for us in verses 7–10.

DAY 5—BEGIN IN PRAYER

1. Read James 5.

2. What are the major points contained in this chapter?

3. What encouragement do you receive?

4. What promises do you find?

5. What warnings are written that we must heed?

JAMES 1–5 REVIEW — LESSON #20

6. What is it that causes us to be able to endure the hardships of this world?

7. How are we instructed to care for the needs of one another in the Body of Christ? **How are you personally making a difference in caring for the Body?**

DAY 6—BEGIN IN PRAYER

1. Read James 1–5.

2. Choose two of the following topics and share how your life has been affected this year through the study of James:

   Trials

   Temptation to sin

   Being a doer of the Word

   Respecting of persons

   The tongue

   Wisdom

JAMES 1–5 REVIEW — LESSON #20

Prayer

Planning for tomorrow

Misuse of riches

Patiently enduring

Ask the Lord to make you a "doer of the Word," controlled by His Spirit and guided by His Word, as you wait patiently for His soon return. Praise Him for His love for you that inspired Him to leave you His Word to guide your life. Record your prayer here.

> But be ye doers of the word, and not hearers only, deceiving your own selves. James 1:22

> Be ye also patient; stablish your hearts: for the coming of the Lord draweth nigh. James 5:8

Made in the USA
Columbia, SC
12 July 2019